I0559804

THE TWO SISTERS COOKBOOK

Il Ricettario Delle Due Sorelle

THE TWO SISTERS COOKBOOK
Il Ricettario Delle Due Sorelle

Family, where life begins and love never ends
Famiglia, dove la vita inizia e l'amore non finisce mai

ANGELA ANTONIANA LEPORE HAUN &
MARIA TERESA LEPORE TREPTOW

MANY**SEASONS**PRESS
Mesa, Arizona · 2025

FIRST EDITION

The Two Sisters Cookbook | Il Ricettario Delle Due Sorelle
Family, where life begins and love never ends
Famiglia, dove la vita inizia e l'amore non finisce mai

Published by Many Seasons Press
an Imprint of Multimedia Publishing Project
123 N. Centennial Way, Suite 105
Mesa, Arizona 85201
480-939-9689 | ManySeasonsPress.com

Book designed by Yolie Hernandez
(AZBookDesigner@icloud.com)

Hardback ISBN: 978-1-956203-46-2
Paperback ISBN: 978-1-956203-41-7

Library of Congress Control Number: 2024932103

CONTENTS

v

SEAFOOD | *Frutti di Mare*

SOUPS & SAUCES | *Zuppe e Salse*

VEGETABLES | *Verdura*

CHEESE | *Formaggio Fresco*

INTRODUCTION

I n late 1959, our family embarked on a journey from Lapio, a small town nestled within the city of Avellino in Southern Italy, and arrived in America aboard a ship.

GROWING UP IN THE UNITED STATES, WE always thought about writing a recipe book with the family Italian dishes handed down through the generations. There were no written recipes in those days, just a little bit of this and a pinch of that. Through the years, with many trials and tribulations, we were able to put the recipes together.

Our mom, Maria Eufemia, Dad Angelo, Aunts Carolina and Elena, Uncle Dominic, and other family members who still live in Italy taught us these dishes. Therefore, la *Famiglia* is our inspiration for this recipe book. We learned from them how to put life and love into these dishes. We dedicate this book to all of them and thank them for all they taught us.

Italian dinners are always full of love and laughter. There is always extra food, no matter how many individuals are at the table. Every time we make one of these dishes, we remember the smells and the fun times we had making them. There were always lots of laughs and, at times, arguing about the amount of ingredients to put in, how to prepare a dish, and so forth. Even if we weren't allowed to make them because we were still too young, we watched and learned. Sunday was always pasta day. The aroma from our mom's ragu and a roast in the oven was awesome. We believe that the souls of our ancestors are kept alive through these dishes. They bring love, warmth, flavors, and lots of fond memories when making them.

In addition to our ancestors' dishes, there are new recipes we have created through the years, variations of different American/Italian flavors.

From our home in the southwestern state of Arizona, we hope you enjoy this recipe book as much as we've enjoyed creating it—laughter, love, and a few spirited debates included.

TRADITIONS

CHRISTMAS EVE TRADITION — Since we were children, our Christmas Eve family tradition consisted of a *presepio* (nativity scene) with houses, figures, and trees placed on a large table and decorated, awaiting the birth of Christ. We were not allowed to put the Baby Jesus in the manger until after Midnight Mass or Christmas day. Today, we still observe this tradition. Dad made the little houses that we still use today. He had them shipped from Italy to the United States so we could keep this tradition going. The traditional meal continues with various seafood, spaghetti with vongole, and zeppoles. As the family grew, meat dishes were introduced for those who were not seafood lovers. These recipes are shared in this book except for the eels.

EASTER TRADITION — Pizza Piena and sweet dishes are traditional Easter meals. Mom and Dad would always argue when making the Pizza Piena. Dad always put lots of salami and eggs, and Mom would say he put too much. We could count on that argument every year. It was also made on Holy Thursday, so we could not eat any of the salami as it was a day of fasting. The recipes for these dishes and desserts are shared in this book. We have kept this tradition and still make some of them. Growing up, we also had our traditional lamb dishes, which we got away from as we got older.

. . .

"La *Famiglia* is our inspiration for this recipe book. We learned from them how to put life and love into these dishes. We dedicate this book to all of them and thank them for all they taught us."

. . .

APPETIZERS AND SIDES

Antipasti e Contorni

STUFFED ARTICHOKES | *Carciofi ripieni*

INGREDIENTS

- 4 artichokes
- ½ cup Italian breadcrumbs
- 1 ½ cups shredded mozzarella
- 1 cup grated Parmesan cheese
- ½ cup chopped fresh parsley
- 2 cloves of garlic, minced
- ¼ cup garlic powder
- 1 lemon, quartered
- Freshly ground black pepper
- Olive oil

INSTRUCTIONS

- [ ] Preheat the oven to 375°F.
- [ ] Clean the artichokes and cut them in half.
- [ ] Scoop out the area in the middle of each artichoke, removing what needs to be taken out.
- [ ] Add the artichokes and lemon slices to a large pot filled halfway with water.
- [ ] Bring to a boil, then simmer until the artichokes are tender, approximately 30 minutes to an hour.
- [ ] Remove the artichokes from the pot and let them cool.
- [ ] While the artichokes are cooling, prepare the stuffing.
- [ ] Mix the breadcrumbs, shredded mozzarella, Parmesan cheese, fresh parsley, fresh garlic, and garlic powder in a large bowl—season with black pepper.
- [ ] Pack the breadcrumb mixture into the artichoke leaves.
- [ ] Place the artichokes on their backs and fill the centers with the same mixture.
- [ ] Place the stuffed artichokes in a greased baking dish.
- [ ] Repeat the process for all the artichoke halves and arrange them in the baking dish.
- [ ] Drizzle some olive oil over the top of the artichokes.
- [ ] Cover the baking dish with tin foil and bake for about 45 minutes.
- [ ] Uncover the dish for the remaining time, approximately another 30 minutes.
- [ ] The artichokes are done when they are lightly golden on top.

ASPARAGUS WITH MOZZARELLA | *Asparigi con Mozzarella*

INGREDIENTS

- 1 bunch of nice asparagus, trimmed and washed
- 2 cups of water
- 1 cup of mozzarella
- ¼ cup Parmesan cheese

INSTRUCTIONS

- ☐ Put the water in a medium sauté pan.
- ☐ Add asparagus. Cover and turn the heat on low, simmering until the asparagus is *al dente*.
- ☐ Drain the water.
- ☐ Place the mozzarella and Parmesan cheese over the asparagus.
- ☐ Cover and let it sit for about 5 minutes or until the mozzarella is melted.
- ☐ Serve with your favorite meat.
- ☐ Salt and pepper to taste.

FRIED CAULIFLOWER | *Cavolfiore Fritto*

INGREDIENTS

- 4 eggs
- ½ cup flour (can use potato starch)
- 1 tsp of black ground pepper
- Canola oil
- Salt to taste

INSTRUCTIONS

- ☐ Break the cauliflower into small florets.
- ☐ Place cauliflower into a pan of boiling water. Cook for 5 to 8 minutes or until slightly tender. Remove from heat, drain, and cool.
- ☐ In a small bowl or blender, add the eggs, black pepper, and flour. Blend until the mixture is a little thick. Add more flour if needed.
- ☐ Heat oil in a sauté pan (about 1-inch of oil).
- ☐ Dip the cauliflower into the egg mixture and drop it into hot olive oil.
- ☐ Fry the coated cauliflower in the hot oil until it's golden brown, turning it around so it cooks on all sides.
- ☐ Place the fried cauliflower on paper towels to drain.
- ☐ Place on a serving plate and serve hot.
- ☐ Leftovers can be stored in the fridge. Just place them in an air fryer or oven to reheat.

CABBAGE AND MUSHROOMS | *Cavolo e Funghi*

INGREDIENTS

- 1 small head of cabbage, cleaned, sliced, and blanched
- 1 lb. Baby Bella mushrooms, sliced
- 3 cloves of garlic, sliced
- ¼ cup extra virgin olive oil

INSTRUCTIONS

- ☐ Place the olive oil in a frying pan.
- ☐ Add the garlic and cook until it turns nice and golden.
- ☐ Spoon the garlic out into a small bowl and set it aside.
- ☐ Add the mushrooms to the oil and cook until they are done, ensuring all the water is cooked out.
- ☐ Add 3 cups of cooked cabbage.
- ☐ Cook everything together for about 10 minutes.
- ☐ Add the cooked garlic and simmer for another 5 minutes.
- ☐ Season with salt and pepper to taste.
- ☐ If desired, add red pepper seeds.

CARROT SALAD | *Insalata di Carote*

INGREDIENTS

- 6 large carrots
- ¼ cup olive oil
- 3 tbsp oregano

- 3 cloves of garlic (chopped)
- Red pepper flakes

INSTRUCTIONS

- ☐ Clean carrots and cut them in 1-inch rounds.
- ☐ Boil carrots in a medium-sized pot until they are just about tender.
- ☐ Drain the carrots and place them in a serving bowl.
- ☐ Add the olive oil and toss to coat.
- ☐ Sprinkle in the oregano and garlic, then toss until they are nicely mixed.
- ☐ Add the desired amount of red pepper flakes and toss again.
- ☐ Serve the dish hot or cold.

ENGLISH MUFFIN PIZZA

INGREDIENTS

- 1 (14.5 oz.) can of diced tomatoes in oregano, garlic, and basil
- 1 small onion, chopped
- 1 tbsp olive oil
- 6 English Muffins, cut in half
- 1 (8 oz.) bag of mozzarella
- 1 tsp oregano

Tip: For toppings, you can have mushrooms, pepperoni, or any other desired topping.

INSTRUCTIONS

- ☐ Place the English muffins on a baking dish sprayed with your favorite non-stick spray.
- ☐ Brush a little oil on the bottom of each muffin.
- ☐ Add the diced tomatoes in oregano, garlic, and basil as the sauce.
- ☐ Sprinkle the mozzarella.
- ☐ Add your favorite topping(s).
- ☐ Top each muffin with a small dab of sauce (marinara sauce recipe is on page 45)
- ☐ Cook at 350°F for 20 minutes.

BRUSCHETTA

INGREDIENTS

- 1 package of fresh mozzarella, sliced
- 4 Roma or vine-ripe tomatoes, sliced
- 1 French baguette, sliced and lightly toasted
- Basil leaves (1 leaf for the top of each bruschetta)
- Garlic powder
- Extra virgin olive oil

INSTRUCTIONS

- ☐ Place the sliced bread on a cookie sheet sprayed on the bottom with Pam.
- ☐ Lightly spray olive oil over the top of the bread and sprinkle some garlic powder over it (if desired).
- ☐ Bake in a 350°F oven for about 10-15 minutes. Be careful not to overbake, or the bread will become too hard.
- ☐ Place the sliced toasted bread on a large platter.
- ☐ Add a slice of mozzarella on top of each bread slice.
- ☐ Add a slice of tomato on top of the mozzarella.
- ☐ Place a basil leaf on the top of each bruschetta.
- ☐ Drizzle with olive oil.

STUFFED BELL PEPPERS | Pepperoni Ripieni

INGREDIENTS

- 4 bell peppers (can be a mixture of red, orange, green, and yellow, or all the same)
- 1 cup Parmesan cheese
- ¼ cup diced parsley
- 2 tbsp diced fresh mint
- 4 eggs

- Half a loaf of fresh Italian bread (broken up into small pieces)
- 3 garlic cloves, diced
- Black pepper
- Optional: ½ lb. cooked ground beef
- Marinara sauce (recipe on page 45)

INSTRUCTIONS

THIS RECIPE SERVES 6

- ☐ Preheat the oven to 350°F.
- ☐ Cut the peppers in half, clean them, and set them aside.
- ☐ Add the bread, Parmesan cheese, parsley, mint, garlic, and some black pepper in a bowl.
- ☐ Add the eggs and mix well once all the dry ingredients are mixed. Use your hands if necessary to blend everything together.
- ☐ Place some sauce at the bottom of a baking dish.
- ☐ Take each half pepper and stuff it with the prepared stuffing mixture. Place the stuffed peppers in the baking dish.
- ☐ Repeat this step for all the pepper halves.
- ☐ Pour the remaining sauce over the top of the peppers and around the sides, ensuring that the peppers sit in the sauce.
- ☐ Sprinkle a handful of mozzarella cheese over the top of each pepper.
- ☐ Cover the baking dish with foil and place it in the center of the oven. Bake for one hour.
- ☐ Check the tenderness of the peppers, and if they are still a bit hard, cook for another 15-20 minutes or until they are nice and soft.
- ☐ When serving, spoon some sauce over each pepper.

DESSERTS
Dolci

ALMOND BISCOTTI | *Biscotti alle Mandorle*

INGREDIENTS

- 2 cups sifted unbleached all-purpose flour
- 1 ½ cups of whole/raw almonds (toast in the oven for 10 minutes)
- ¾ cup sugar
- 2 large eggs

- 1 tsp baking powder
- ¼ cup butter (melted)
- ¼ tsp salt
- 1 tsp vanilla extract
- ¼ cup Frangelico liquor (optional)
- Lemon or orange zest (optional)

DIRECTIONS

MAKES ABOUT 2 ½ DOZEN BISCOTTI

- ☐ Place the oven rack in the middle of the oven and heat to 350°F.
- ☐ Line a cookie sheet with parchment paper.
- ☐ Sift flour.
- ☐ Place flour, sugar, baking powder, salt, and nuts in a large bowl. Mix to combine.
- ☐ Mix eggs, butter, and vanilla in another bowl, and whisk to fully combine.
- ☐ Make a well in the center of the dry ingredients and pour egg mixture.
- ☐ Using a rubber spatula, mix and combine until a rough dough forms.
- ☐ Place the dough on a work surface and knead until the dough comes together.
- ☐ Add extra flour sparingly and only if necessary.
- ☐ Form the dough into the size of a loaf of bread.

- ☐ Place it onto the cookie sheet and lightly press with fingers to flatten it a bit.
- ☐ Bake for 25 minutes. Reverse the pan halfway through. The dough will be firm to the touch and just slightly browned.
- ☐ Remove from the oven and lower the oven to 300°F.
- ☐ Let the dough cool on a cookie sheet for 15 minutes.
- ☐ Place the dough on a cutting board.
- ☐ Using a serrated knife, slice the dough into biscotti bars diagonally about ½-inch thick.
- ☐ Put them back on the cookie sheet with cut side down, and place back in over for 15 minutes.
- ☐ Flip the cookies and place them back in the oven for another 15 minutes.
- ☐ Take them out and let them cool on a rack.
- ☐ Place cookies in an airtight container.

11

ALMOND SOFT COOKIES | *Biscotti morbidi alle mandorle*

INGREDIENTS

- 1 cup shortening
- 1 cup sugar
- ½ cup finely ground almonds
- 1 tsp almond extract
- 1 egg, beaten
- 1 tsp vanilla
- 1 ½ tbsp baking powder

- 1 egg yolk
- 2 ½ cups sifted unbleached all-purpose flour
- ½ tsp salt
- 1 tbsp water
- 30 blanched almond halves
- Lemon zest (optional)

INSTRUCTIONS

- ☐ Preheat oven to 350°F.
- ☐ Grease the baking sheets or use parchment paper on the baking sheets. Set them aside.
- ☐ Mix the shortening and sugar in a large bowl until smooth.
- ☐ Add egg, ground almonds, and almond extract.
- ☐ In a medium bowl, mix flour, baking powder, and salt.
- ☐ Gradually add the dry mixture to the egg mixture. Mix well. The dough will be stiff.
- ☐ Shape dough into small balls. Place balls about 2 inches apart on a baking sheet.
- ☐ Press an almond half onto each ball and flatten them with the palm of your hand.
- ☐ Mix egg yolk and water in a small cup. Brush each cookie with the egg.
- ☐ Bake for about 20 minutes or until golden brown.

BUTTER COOKIES | *Biscotti al burro*

INGREDIENTS

- 1 ¾ cups softened butter
- ½ cup white sugar
- 2 egg yolks
- 1 ¾ cups sifted unbleached all-purpose flour
- Maraschino cherries for the top
- ¼ cup lemon or orange zest (optional)
- ¼ cup crushed almonds (optional)
- 1 egg yolk
- 1 tsp water

INSTRUCTIONS

MAKES ABOUT 3 DOZEN COOKIES

- ☐ Preheat the oven to 350°F.
- ☐ In a medium bowl, cream the butter, white sugar, and egg yolks. (Add the zest and crushed almonds if using).
- ☐ Sift the flour and mix in flour a little bit at a time until soft and dough forms. Refrigerate the dough for 10 minutes.
- ☐ Roll dough into 1-inch balls.
- ☐ Flatten each cookie a little bit using a spatula.
- ☐ Cut a cherry in half and press on top of each ball.
- ☐ Mix the egg yolk and water. Brush the mixture on top of the cookie before baking.
- ☐ Bake for 8-10 minutes or until golden brown on the bottom.
- ☐ Remove the cookies and place on wire rack to cool.

13

BOW TIE COOKIES | *Farfallette*

INGREDIENTS

- 3 large eggs
- ½ cup sugar
- ¼ cup white wine
- 2 ¾ cups sifted unbleached all-purpose flour
- Pinch of salt
- Oil for frying
- For dusting: confectioners' sugar or honey with colored sprinkles

INSTRUCTIONS

- ☐ Place eggs, sugar, salt, and wine in a large bowl.
- ☐ Mix until nicely blended.
- ☐ Add 1 cup of flour and mix well.
- ☐ Add the remaining flour and mix until a sticky dough is formed.
- ☐ Form the dough into a ball with your hands.
- ☐ Cover and refrigerate for an hour.
- ☐ Remove from the fridge and cut the dough in half.
- ☐ Roll half of the dough on a floured board until it is nice and thin. A pasta roller machine can be used.
- ☐ Using a knife or a fluted pastry wheel, cut it into strips 6-7 inches long.
- ☐ Make a small cut towards the end of each strip. Then, place the opposite end through the slit and pull through to make a ribbon. Repeat until all the dough is used.
- ☐ Heat up some oil (about 2 inches) in a pot or deep fryer until it is nice and hot.
- ☐ Drop the dough into the hot oil and fry them until they are puffed and light golden brown.
- ☐ Remove them with a strainer and place them on a paper towel to cool.
- ☐ Once cooled, place them on a serving dish.
- ☐ Sprinkle them with honey and colored sprinkles, or dust them with confectioners' sugar.

STRAWBERRY CAKE | *Torta di Fragole*

INGREDIENTS

- ▸ **1 package of strawberry cake mix**
- ▸ **1 lb. of strawberries (half sliced and half whole)**
- ▸ **2 packages of whipped cream**

INSTRUCTIONS

- ☐ Mix the cake according to the directions on the package.
- ☐ Bake the cake in two separate layer pans.
- ☐ Place the first layer of cake on a serving dish.
- ☐ Spread a generous layer of whipped cream.
- ☐ Add the sliced strawberries to this first layer.
- ☐ Place the second layer of cake on top.
- ☐ Spread whipped cream all over it.
- ☐ Add sliced and whole strawberries to the top.
- ☐ Put it in the refrigerator to chill for a bit.

CANNOLI FILLING

INGREDIENTS

- 2 cups ricotta cheese
- ¾ cup powdered sugar
- 1 tsp ground cinnamon
- ½ tsp vanilla
- ¼ cup heavy cream
- 1 lemon

For the ends of each cannoli, you can use semi-sweet chocolate chips, ground pistachios, half a maraschino cherry, or confetti. You can use the same items for all or use different items on each end for a mix of different flavors.

INSTRUCTIONS

- ☐ Sift in the powdered sugar, cinnamon, and vanilla.
- ☐ Whisk the ricotta in a medium-sized bowl until nice and smooth.
- ☐ Beat the heavy cream in a separate bowl or using an electric mixer with the whisk attachment until it is fairly stiff.
- ☐ Using a rubber spatula, gently fold the cream into the ricotta mixture.
- ☐ Zest the lemon and stir it into the ricotta mixture.
- ☐ Refrigerate the mixture for an hour or so before filling the cannoli shells.

FILLING THE CANNOLI'S

- ☐ Use a pastry bag without a tip to fill the shells. If you don't have a pastry bag, use a Ziplock bag with a small cut at the tip.
- ☐ Fill the cannoli shells from both ends so the ricotta fills the whole shell.
- ☐ Place your choice of chocolate chips, ground pistachios, maraschino cherry, or confetti on each end of the cannoli.
- ☐ Dust lightly with powdered sugar.
- ☐ Put them on a serving tray.
- ☐ Fill the cannoli just before serving. If you fill them too early, the shells will get soft.

Tip: For cannoli shells, you can either purchase them from a store or make your own shells. The shells pictured were made with the Pizzella maker. The Pizzella recipe on page 24 and the homemade cannoli shells recipe is on page 22.

CHEESECAKE

INGREDIENTS

CRUST

- 1 ¾ cups graham cracker crumbs
- 6 tbsp salted butter, melted
- 2 tbsp sugar (optional, as the cracker crumbs are already sweet)

INSTRUCTIONS

- ☐ Preheat the oven to 325°F.
- ☐ Line a 9-inch springform pan with parchment paper at the bottom and grease both sides.
- ☐ Combine the crust ingredients in a small bowl. Press the mixture into the bottom of the pan.
- ☐ Bake the crust for 10-15 minutes, then set it aside.
- ☐ Cover the outside of the pan with aluminum foil to prevent water from the water bath from getting into the pan. Set aside the prepared pan.

INGREDIENTS

FILLING

- 40 oz. cream cheese (5-8 oz. packages), softened
- 1 ½ cups of sugar
- 3 tbsp sifted unbleached all-purpose flour
- ¼ cup lemon zest (reduce if you don't desire too much lemon)
- 3 tbsp orange zest
- 4 tsp vanilla
- ½ cup heavy cream
- 5 large eggs, room temperature
- 2 large egg yolks, room temperature

INSTRUCTIONS

- ☐ Reduce the oven temperature to 300°F.
- ☐ In a large bowl, beat the cream cheese, sugar, and flour at low speed until combined.
- ☐ Add the lemon and orange zest and vanilla. Beat at low speed until combined.
- ☐ Add the heavy cream and beat at low speed until combined.
- ☐ Add the eggs and egg yolks individually. Beat each one at low speed until everything is combined.
- ☐ Pour the cheesecake batter into the crust. The pan will be pretty full.
- ☐ Place the springform pan in a larger pan. Fill the outside pan with enough water to go about halfway up the sides of the springform pan.
- ☐ Bake for 2 hours.
- ☐ Turn the oven off and leave the door closed for 30 minutes.
- ☐ Crack open the oven door for another 30 minutes.
- ☐ Remove the springform pan from the other pan and refrigerate overnight.
- ☐ Remove the cake from the springform pan and place it on a serving dish.
- ☐ Serve plain or with your favorite toppings.

EASTER GRAIN PIE | Pizza con Grano

INGREDIENTS

PIE CRUST

- ▸ **4 cups sifted unbleached all-purpose flour**
- ▸ **5 tsp baking powder**
- ▸ **1 cup sugar**
- ▸ **½ cup shortening, chilled**
- ▸ **4 eggs, slightly beaten**
- ▸ **1 tsp vanilla**
- ▸ **1 tbsp milk**
- ▸ **1 tbsp lemon zest**
- ▸ **1 tbsp orange zest**

INSTRUCTIONS

- ☐ Combine the flour, baking powder, and sugar.
- ☐ Cut in ½ cup plus 1 tbsp of chilled shortening until the mixture resembles coarse crumbs.
- ☐ Mix in the 4 beaten eggs, vanilla, lemon zest, orange zest, and milk.
- ☐ Mix well and form a dough.
- ☐ Divide the dough into 4 balls. Wrap each ball in plastic wrap and chill for 30 minutes.
- ☐ Knead out the 2 bottom halves of each pie dish on a floured board. Use the rest of the dough to cut lattice strips for the tops of the pies.
- ☐ Shield the edges of the crust, all the way around, with foil and place the pies in the oven.
- ☐ Bake for 45 minutes or until the crust is golden.
- ☐ Remove the foil and bake for another 20-30 minutes. Insert a toothpick in the center, and it should come out dry.
- ☐ Cool the pies completely, then refrigerate before serving.
- ☐ Optional garnish: Sprinkle with confectioners' sugar before serving.

INGREDIENTS

FILLING

- 5 cups of water
- ½ cup whole wheat berries (or farro)
- 6 eggs
- 1 cup white sugar
- 1 (8 oz.) package of dried candied fruits (optional)
- 1 ½ lbs. whole ricotta cheese
- 1 tsp vanilla extract
- ½ tsp ground cinnamon
- 1 tbsp lemon zest
- 1 tbsp orange zest
- 1 tsp salt
- 2 pastries for 9-inch top pies
- 2 tbsp confectioners' sugar for dusting (optional)

INSTRUCTIONS

- ☐ Preheat oven to 375°F.
- ☐ Bring water to a boil in a large saucepan. Add the wheat berries (or farro) and allow them to boil for 40 minutes.
- ☐ While the wheat is cooking, beat the eggs in a large bowl, gradually adding the sugar. Mix in the ricotta cheese, vanilla extract, cinnamon, lemon zest, and orange zest. If desired, mix in the dried candied fruits.
- ☐ When the wheat berries (or farro) are ready, drain them in a colander and rinse with warm water. Set aside.
- ☐ Add ¾ cup of cooked wheat berries (or farro) into the ricotta mixture. Add the rest of the cooked wheat berries (or farro) and mix again.
- ☐ Line two 9-inch pie pans with pastry. Cut the remaining pastry into strips for the lattice top of the pies.
- ☐ Spoon half of the filling into each pan. Cover with pastry strips to form a lattice top. Crimp the edges.
- ☐ Bake for 45 minutes or until the crust is golden brown. Allow the pies to cool at room temperature.
- ☐ Chill the pies overnight before serving. Sprinkle with confectioners' sugar when serving. Store any leftovers in the refrigerator.

HOMEMADE CANNOLI SHELLS

INGREDIENTS

- 2 cups of all-purpose flour (sifted)
- 2 tbsp light brown sugar
- 3 tbsp unsalted butter, cold, cut into cubes
- ¼ tsp salt
- ½ cup Marsala wine
- 3 large eggs, beaten and divided
- Vegetable oil for frying

INSTRUCTIONS

- ☐ Whisk together the sifted flour, light brown sugar, and salt in a large mixing bowl.
- ☐ Add the cold butter to the mixture.
- ☐ Using a pastry cutter or your hands, work the butter into the flour mixture until it becomes crumbly.

- [ ] Add the Marsala wine and 1 beaten egg. Stir until well combined and the dough comes together.
- [ ] Form the dough into a flat disc and wrap it in plastic wrap.
- [ ] Refrigerate the dough for at least an hour.
- [ ] Remove half of the dough from the refrigerator and place it on a lightly floured work surface.
- [ ] Roll the dough with a rolling pin until it is thin, about ¼-inch thick or less.
- [ ] Cut out circles from the dough using a floured 4-inch round cookie or biscuit cutter.
- [ ] Repeat the rolling and cutting process until all the dough is used.
- [ ] Wrap one circle of dough around a metal cannoli tube at a time.
- [ ] Seal the overlapping edge with the remaining beaten egg and press the dough together gently to seal.
- [ ] Fill a large, heavy pot or Dutch oven with a few inches of vegetable oil and heat it over medium-high heat.
- [ ] Using long tongs or a metal spider strainer, carefully place the dough-wrapped molds into the hot oil and fry for about 3 minutes or until golden brown.
- [ ] Fry only a few shells at a time, turning the molds to ensure even cooking.
- [ ] Remove the shells from the oil with the tongs and place them on a paper towel-lined surface to cool.
- [ ] Repeat the frying process until all the shells are done.
- [ ] Once the shells have cooled, gently squeeze and twist the molds to remove them from the pastry shells.
- [ ] Make sure the shells are completely cooled before filling them with cream.

Tip: Be careful when handling, as they can break easily. Find the filling recipe on page 16. Cannoli forms made by Uncle Dominic.

TARALLI

INGREDIENTS:

- 1½ pounds all-purpose flour
- 1 cup extra-virgin olive oil
- 1 cup lukewarm water, or as much as needed
- ½ cup white wine
- Optional flavorings add red pepper flakes, ground black pepper, or fennel seeds

INSTRUCTIONS:

- ☐ Preheat oven to 400°F.
- ☐ Place the flour on a clean work surface. Make a well in the center and add the olive oil, wine, and water.
- ☐ Combine the ingredients and knead until a smooth, even dough forms. If needed, add more water gradually while kneading.
- ☐ Cut off a small portion of the dough and roll it into a log about ½ inch thick.
- ☐ Cut the log into 5-inch pieces. Shape each piece into a ring by pinching the opposite ends together.
- ☐ Repeat with the remaining dough.
- ☐ Bring a large pot of water to a boil. Drop a few taralli at a time into the water and boil for about 1 minute, or until they float to the surface.
- ☐ Stir gently to prevent sticking.
- ☐ Remove the taralli with a slotted spoon and place them on a clean dishcloth to dry.
- ☐ Line a baking tray with parchment paper. Arrange the taralli on the tray and bake for about 10 minutes, or until golden brown on one side.
- ☐ Turn the taralli over and bake the other side until equally golden.

ITALIAN PIZZELLE

INGREDIENTS

- 6 eggs
- ½ cup vegetable oil
- 1 tsp vanilla
- 1 tsp anise
- 2 tsp baking powder
- 3 cups sifted unbleached all-purpose flour
- 1 ½ cups sugar
- Confectioners' sugar
- Lemon zest (optional)

INSTRUCTIONS

MAKES ABOUT 70 PIZZELLES

- ☐ Turn on the Pizzelle maker and get it ready to cook the pizzelles.
- ☐ Beat the eggs until smooth.
- ☐ Add the oil, vanilla, and anise to the beaten eggs.
- ☐ Place the flour, baking powder, and sugar in a separate bowl. Mix well.
- ☐ Add the dry ingredients to the egg mixture.
- ☐ The mixture will be sticky and stiff. Add a teaspoon of water to adjust the consistency if it is too stiff.
- ☐ Place a teaspoon of dough on each pizzelle grill. Close the lid and cook for about 20 seconds.
- ☐ Briefly open the grill to check if the pizzelle is done. It should be firm and have a light golden color. Place the cooked pizzelle on a cookie sheet to cool.
- ☐ Repeat this process until all the dough is used.
- ☐ Sprinkle the pizzelles with powdered sugar. Stack them on a platter and serve.
- ☐ Place any leftovers in a covered dish or plastic container. These will keep for quite a long time.

OPTIONAL CHOCOLATE

Add ½ cup of unsweetened cocoa to the batter or melt 6 ounces of semi-sweet chocolate and mix in the batter.

CANNOLI SHELLS MADE FROM PIZZELLE

- ☐ Use the above recipe to make the pizzelle batter.
- ☐ Instead of laying them flat, roll the pizzelles into cannoli shells.
- ☐ When ready to serve, stuff the cannoli shells with cannoli filling.

ITALIAN RUM CAKE | *torta al Rum*

THIS CAKE HAS THREE PARTS:

1. **The cake**
2. **The cream filling**
3. **Assembling the cake**

Note: This cake takes a few hours to make, so give yourself plenty of time to prepare it and gather all the necessary ingredients. It is also recommended to refrigerate the cake and custard cream filling separately and assemble them the following day. It's best to have everything cooled off and ready for assembly instead of trying to do everything in one day.

INGREDIENTS

ITALIAN SPONGE CAKE:

- **5 egg yolks**
- **5 egg whites**
- **1 tbsp vanilla**
- **1 ½ cups sugar**

- **1 ¼ cups pastry flour**
- **1 tsp freshly grated lemon zest**
- **½ tsp vanilla**

INSTRUCTIONS

- ☐ Place the egg yolks and sugar in a mixing bowl. Beat until the mixture becomes very thick and has a nice lemony color.

- ☐ Gradually add the pastry flour to the egg mixture, gently mixing it in.

- ☐ Add the vanilla extract and freshly grated lemon.

- ☐ In another small bowl, beat the egg whites until they form stiff peaks but are not dry.

- ☐ Add the beaten egg whites slowly to the egg mixture, gently blending them together.

- ☐ Pour the cake batter into three 9-inch cake pans that have been lined with parchment paper or greased and floured.

- ☐ Bake at 375°F for about 20 minutes or until a toothpick inserted in the center comes out dry. The baking time may vary depending on your oven.

- ☐ Remove the pans from the oven and set them aside to cool.

- ☐ Once the cakes have cooled, take them out of the pans and wrap each one in tin foil. Place them in the refrigerator.

INGREDIENTS

LEMON CUSTARD CREAM FILLING | *RIPIENO DI CREMA*

- 3 tbsp regular sugar or confectioners' sugar
- 3 egg yolks
- $\frac{1}{3}$ cup sifted unbleached all-purpose flour

- $\frac{1}{2}$ tsp vanilla extract
- 2 cups whole milk
- 1 tbsp butter
- 1 lemon rind

INSTRUCTIONS

- ☐ Place the sugar, egg yolks, flour, lemon rind, and vanilla extract in a saucepan and mix them together.
- ☐ In a separate saucepan, scald the milk.
- ☐ Pour the milk very slowly over the egg yolk mixture, beating constantly with a rotary beater until all the milk is incorporated. Then, switch to stirring with a wooden spoon until the mixture comes to a boil.
- ☐ Stir the mixture for a few more minutes, then remove the pan from the heat. Stir in the butter and mix well.
- ☐ Pour the mixture into a bowl and let it cool. Stir occasionally to prevent skin from forming on the top.
- ☐ Once the mixture has cooled, remove the lemon rind, cover it with plastic wrap, and place it in the refrigerator.

INGREDIENTS

CHOCOLATE CUSTARD CREAM FILLING | *RIPIENO DI CREMA PASTICCERA AL CIOCCOLATO*

- 1 tbsp regular sugar or confectioners' sugar
- 3 egg yolks
- $\frac{1}{3}$ cup sifted unbleached all-purpose flour

- $\frac{1}{2}$ tsp vanilla extract
- 2 cups whole milk
- 1 tbsp butter
- 2 tbsp cocoa powder

INSTRUCTIONS

- ☐ Place the sugar, egg yolks, flour, cocoa powder, and vanilla extract in a saucepan and mix them together.

- ☐ In a separate saucepan, scald the milk.

- ☐ Pour the milk very slowly over the egg yolk mixture, beating constantly with a rotary beater until all the milk is incorporated. Then, stir with a wooden spoon until it comes to a boil. Stir a few more minutes, then remove the pan from the heat.

- ☐ Stir in the butter and mix well. Pour the mixture into a bowl and let it cool. Stir occasionally to prevent skin from forming on the top. Once it is cooled, cover it with plastic wrap and place it in the refrigerator.

RUM SPREAD

▸ **1 cup of light or dark rum, pour it into a small bowl**

INSTRUCTIONS

CAKE ASSEMBLY

- ☐ Place the first layer of the cake crust side down and brush the rum over the cake back and forth until the layer is covered.

- ☐ Top this layer with the lemon custard cream.

- ☐ Lay the second layer of the cake on top of the lemon custard. Brush the layer with rum going back and forth until it is covered.

- ☐ Top this layer with the chocolate custard.

☐ Brush the top layer with rum before laying it on top of the chocolate custard layer.

☐ Lay the last layer of the cake on top of the chocolate custard.

Note: The top of the cake can be sprinkled with confectioners' sugar. You can add sliced almonds between the layers or your choice of thinly sliced fruits, etc. You can also make a whipped cream topping.

WHIPPED CREAM TOPPING

▸ **1 pint heavy whipping cream**
▸ **4 tbsp powdered sugar**

INSTRUCTIONS

☐ Place the whipping cream in the freezer for about 10 minutes.

☐ Combine the sugar and whipping cream with an electric mixer and whip until stiff peaks form.

☐ Decorate the top of the cake (and sides if desired), and add sliced almonds and cherry topping if desired.

JAM FILLED BISCOTTI | *Biscotti ripieni di marmellata*

INGREDIENTS

BISCOTTI DOUGH

- 5 cups sifted unbleached all-purpose flour
- 1 cup sugar
- 1 ½ tbsp baking powder

- 4 eggs
- 1 orange, juice and zest
- ½ cup milk
- 1/3 cup shortening

INSTRUCTIONS

MAKES ABOUT 6 DOZEN BISCOTTI

- ☐ Sift the flour into a mixing bowl.
- ☐ Mix all the dry ingredients in a large bowl.
- ☐ Combine the eggs, shortening, and remaining wet ingredients into the flour mixture.
- ☐ Combine all the ingredients and form them into a ball. The dough will be soft.
- ☐ Wrap the dough in plastic wrap and refrigerate it for 1 hour.

- ☐ Roll the dough into long strips similar to a strudel.
- ☐ Place the dough on a cookie sheet covered with parchment paper.
- ☐ Spread the filling in the center and overlap, tucking the seam under.
- ☐ Bake at 375°F for 12-15 minutes.
- ☐ Let the loaves cool.
- ☐ Once cooled, you can slice them into biscotti.
- ☐ You can add powdered sugar or a lemon juice frosting on top.

FILLING

- Any kind of jam can be used for the filling. You don't have to use the same jam, it can be one roll with one and another with a different jam.

FROSTING (OPTIONAL):

- 1 cup confectioners' sugar
- 3 ½ tbsp milk

- 2 drops of lemon juice
- 2 drops of extract (your choice)

Tip: Mix all the ingredients for the frosting. Drizzle or brush the frosting on the tops of the loaves before cutting.

RICOTTA PIE | *torta di Ricotta*

INGREDIENTS

FILLING

- 12 eggs
- 2 cups white sugar
- 2 tsp vanilla extract

- 3 lbs. whole ricotta cheese
- ¼ cup lemon zest
- ¼ cup orange zest

INSTRUCTIONS

- ☐ Beat eggs, sugar, and vanilla in a large bowl.
- ☐ Stir in ricotta cheese.
- ☐ Add lemon and orange zest.
- ☐ Mix well.
- ☐ Set aside.
- ☐ Heat oven to 350°F.

INGREDIENTS

CRUST

- **4 cups all-purpose flour, sifted**
- **1 cup white sugar**
- **5 tsp baking powder**
- **1 tbsp shortening, chilled**

- **4 eggs, lightly beaten**
- **1 tsp vanilla extract**
- **2 tbsp lemon and orange zest**

INSTRUCTIONS

- ☐ Grease 2 9-inch deep-dish pie plates. Set aside.
- ☐ Combine flour, sugar, and baking powder in a large bowl,
- ☐ Cut in the shortening until the mixture resembles coarse crumbs.
- ☐ Mix in beaten eggs, vanilla, orange, and lemon zest.
- ☐ Divide the dough into 4 balls, wrap them in plastic, and chill for 30 minutes.
- ☐ Roll out 2 dough balls and line the bottom and sides of each prepared pie plate. Don't make the crust too thick.
- ☐ Pour the ricotta mixture filling into each pie evenly.
- ☐ Roll out the other 2 dough balls.
- ☐ Cut ½-inch strips using a paring knife or a fluted pastry wheel.
- ☐ Lay the strips in the center of each pie, then lay the others and lay them across, forming an "X" on the top.
- ☐ Fold the edges of the crust and lightly press down with a fork.
- ☐ Arrange foil around the edges of the crust to prevent burning while baking.
- ☐ Bake for 20-30 minutes; then remove the foil.
- ☐ Continue to bake for another 20 minutes or until a knife or toothpick comes out clean when inserted.
- ☐ Cool the pies on a wire rack. Refrigerate until ready to serve.

STRUFFOLI

INGREDIENTS

- 3 cups sifted unbleached all-purpose flour (we prefer King Arthur)
- 4 eggs, beaten
- ¼ cup butter
- ½ cup white sugar
- ½ tsp salt
- 2 tsp baking powder
- 2 tbsp lemon zest
- 2 tbsp orange zest
- 2 cups honey
- Extra virgin olive oil or canola oil
- Multi-colored candy sprinkles

INSTRUCTIONS

- ☐ Melt the butter and add it to the beaten eggs.
- ☐ Mix together in a large bowl 2 ½ cups of flour.
- ☐ Add sugar, baking powder, lemon zest, orange zest, and salt.
- ☐ Mix with a wooden spoon, then start mixing with your hands until the dough no longer sticks to the bowl's sides.
- ☐ Add the remaining ½ cup of flour as needed.
- ☐ Knead the dough on a floured surface until it is no longer sticky.
- ☐ Break off pieces of dough and roll them into small ropes.
- ☐ Cut the ropes into pieces about ¼-inch long and roll these pieces into little balls. Set them aside.
- ☐ Heat up the oil, about 2-inch deep, in a frying pan.
- ☐ Fry the balls until golden brown. Drain them on paper towels.
- ☐ Bring the honey to a slight boil in a large saucepan over medium heat. Let it gently boil for about 3 minutes.
- ☐ Slowly add the fried balls to the honey, stirring gently with a wooden spoon until they become a nice golden color.
- ☐ Remove the balls from the honey with a slotted spoon or slotted ladle and place them in a deep dish or mound them on a platter.
- ☐ Sprinkle them with the multi-colored candy sprinkles.
- ☐ Let them cool before serving.

THUMBPRINT COOKIES

INGREDIENTS

- 1 ¾ cups sifted unbleached all-purpose flour
- ½ tsp baking powder
- ½ tsp salt
- ¾ cup (1 ½ sticks) butter (softened)

- ½ cup sugar
- 1 large egg
- 1 tsp vanilla
- Assorted jams
- 1 ½ to 2 cups of crushed hazelnuts, almonds or pecans (your choice)

INSTRUCTIONS

- ☐ Preheat the oven to 350°F.
- ☐ Line two baking sheets with parchment paper.
- ☐ Mix the flour, baking powder, and salt in a large bowl.
- ☐ In another bowl, beat the butter and sugar until nice and fluffy.
- ☐ Beat in the egg and vanilla.
- ☐ Add the butter mixture to the flour mixture, baking powder, and salt.
- ☐ Using a small scoop, make 1-inch balls.

- ☐ Roll them in the crushed hazelnuts.
- ☐ Place the balls on the prepared baking sheet.
- ☐ Press a thumbprint into the center of each ball, about ½-inch deep.
- ☐ Fill the hole with a spoonful of jam.
- ☐ You may sprinkle more nuts on top if desired.
- ☐ Bake until the edges of the cookies are golden, about 15 minutes.
- ☐ Cool the cookies on baking racks.

34

CHOCOLATE CHIP WALNUT COOKIES |
Biscotti al Cioccolato e Noci

INGREDIENTS

- 1 cup light brown sugar
- 1 cup sugar
- ½ cup butter (softened)
- ½ cup vegetable oil
- 2 eggs
- 1 tsp baking soda
- 1 tsp baking powder
- 1 tsp vanilla extract
- 3 cups sifted unbleached all-purpose flour
- 1 cup milk chocolate chips
- ¾ cup chopped walnuts

INSTRUCTIONS

- ☐ Preheat the oven to 350°F.
- ☐ Cream together the butter, oil and sugars in a stand mixer (or with a hand mixer in a bowl).
- ☐ Add the eggs and beat until fluffy.
- ☐ Add the baking soda, baking powder, vanilla, and flour, and mix well.
- ☐ Fold in the chopped walnuts and chocolate chips.
- ☐ Scoop the dough with a cookie scoop or spoon and roll it into a ball.
- ☐ Place the dough balls on a lightly greased baking sheet.
- ☐ Bake for 8-18 minutes.

35

ITALIAN WEDDING COOKIES | *Biscotti nuziali Italiani*

INGREDIENTS

- 1 cup all-purpose flour or cake flour
- 1 ½ cups walnuts (finely chopped)
- 2 tbsp granulated sugar
- 1 tsp vanilla extract
- 1 stick of butter (softened)
- Powdered sugar

INSTRUCTIONS

- ☐ Mix all the dry ingredients (flour, walnuts, sugar) in a large bowl.
- ☐ Add the vanilla extract.
- ☐ Add the butter in little pieces.
- ☐ Combine everything together with your (clean) hands until the mixture looks coarse with nut bits in it.
- ☐ Chill the dough for at least 30 minutes or even overnight.
- ☐ Preheat the oven to 300°F.
- ☐ Line a baking sheet with parchment paper.
- ☐ Form the dough into small balls no larger than a walnut.
- ☐ Place the balls on the cookie sheet, spaced at least an inch apart from each other.
- ☐ Bake the cookies for 35 minutes.
- ☐ Take them out of the oven and roll them in powdered sugar when they are still warm to the touch but cool enough to handle. (Note: If you try to touch them too early while they are still hot, they will crumble, so ensure they are warm.
- ☐ Set the cookies aside on a rack to cool completely.

ITALIAN DOUGHNUTS | *Zeppole*

INGREDIENTS

- 1 packet of dry yeast
- ¼ teaspoon granulated sugar
- 1 ½ tsp salt
- 1 ¾ cups warm water (you can use ½ cup milk and 1 ½ cups water)
- 3 cups sifted unbleached all-purpose flour
- Vegetable oil for frying
- Powdered sugar or cinnamon and sugar for dusting the fried zeppole

INSTRUCTIONS

- ☐ In a large bowl, stir together the yeast, sugar, salt, and warm water until dissolved.
- ☐ Let this mixture stand for about 10 minutes.
- ☐ Stir in the flour until well mixed.
- ☐ Cover the bowl with plastic wrap and let the dough rise until double in size. The dough will be sticky.
- ☐ In a large pan, heat about 2-3 inches of oil.
- ☐ Carefully drop rounded tablespoons of the dough into the hot oil.
- ☐ Fry the dough until it turns a nice golden color. You can fry 4-5 dough balls, depending on the pan size.
- ☐ Place the fried zeppole on a paper towel-lined rack or pan.
- ☐ While the zeppole are still warm, you can roll them in sugar mixed with cinnamon or dust them with powdered sugar.
- ☐ Serve the zeppole warm.

MEATS

Carni

CHICKEN CACCIATORE | *Pollo Cacciatore*

INGREDIENTS

- 6 chicken legs and 6 chicken thighs (you can also use breast, but they tend to be drier)
- 1 can crushed Cento tomatoes
- 1 lb. of cremini, white mushrooms, or baby bella mushrooms, cleaned and sliced
- 2 cups vermouth
- ½ cup diced onion
- 1 bay leaf
- 1 tsp oregano
- ½ tsp sage
- ½ tsp rosemary (ground or powder)
- 4 garlic cloves, diced
- ¼ cup extra virgin olive oil

INSTRUCTIONS

- ☐ Place the olive oil in a large, heavy sauté pan. Heat the oil over medium-high heat.
- ☐ Add the chicken pieces to the pan and sauté them just until they turn golden brown. Once done, place the chicken on a plate and set it aside.
- ☐ Add the diced garlic and onion in the same pan, and sauté them over medium heat until the onion becomes tender.
- ☐ Pour in the vermouth and simmer until it is reduced by half.
- ☐ Add the crushed tomatoes, oregano, sage, and rosemary to the pan.
- ☐ Return the chicken to this mixture and let it simmer until it is nice and tender.
- ☐ Just before the chicken is fully cooked, add the sliced mushrooms and let everything cook for about 20 minutes longer.
- ☐ Add salt and pepper to taste.
- ☐ Remove the bay leaf before serving.

Serving suggestion: Serve the cooked chicken and mushroom mixture over linguini or angel hair pasta, or enjoy it by itself with pasta as a side. Rice can also be used as an alternative to pasta.

CHICKEN CUTLETS | Cotolette di Pollo

INGREDIENTS

- 2 large chicken breasts
- 4 eggs
- ½ cup grated Parmesan cheese (divided into two ¼ cups)
- 1 ½ cups Italian breadcrumbs
- ¼ cup chopped parsley
- 1 tbsp garlic powder
- 1 cup sliced fresh mushrooms or 1 large can of canned mushrooms
- ¼ cup milk
- ¼ jar of pepperoncini (16 oz. jar, use half)
- 1 large clove of garlic (sliced)
- ½ cup extra virgin olive oil or canola oil
- Pam (cooking spray)
- Salt and pepper to taste

INSTRUCTIONS

- ☐ Preheat the oven to 350°F.
- ☐ Fillet the chicken breasts into 3-4 slices, depending on thickness. Pound and set them aside.
- ☐ In a bowl, whisk the eggs, add milk, and ¼ cup of Parmesan cheese. Whisk until nicely blended (set aside).
- ☐ Mix breadcrumbs, garlic powder, chopped parsley, and ¼ cup of Parmesan cheese in another bowl. Mix well.
- ☐ Dip the chicken in the egg mixture, then in the breadcrumb mixture, pressing to adhere.
- ☐ Preheat oil in a large skillet over medium heat.
- ☐ Gently add the chicken and cook 2-3 minutes per side until golden brown. Place the cooked chicken in a dish lined with a paper towel. Set aside.
- ☐ Place the cooked chicken in a baking dish sprayed with Pam.
- ☐ Add garlic and mushrooms to the skillet and cook for 4-5 minutes.
- ☐ Add the pepperoncini and cook for another 3-5 minutes. Add some pepperoncini water from the jar and a couple of tablespoons.
- ☐ Once the mixture is thoroughly heated and well stirred, pour it over the chicken cutlets.
- ☐ Bake at 350°F for about 10-15 minutes.
- ☐ When done, remove the dish from the oven and serve hot.

ITALIAN STYLE BAKED CHICKEN | *Pollo al forno all'Italiana*

INGREDIENTS

- 1 whole chicken, cut into pieces
- 1 good-sized onion, sliced
- ½ cup fresh parsley, diced
- 1 large russet potato
- 1 lb. mushrooms, cleaned and sliced
- 1 large sweet potato or yam
- 1 ½ cups frozen peas
- 1 cup low-sodium chicken broth
- ½ cup grated Parmesan cheese

INSTRUCTIONS

- ☐ Preheat the oven to 350°F.
- ☐ Clean the chicken and place it on the bottom of a baking pan or Dutch oven.
- ☐ Add the chicken broth.
- ☐ Clean the potatoes and cut them into slices. Place them on top and around the chicken.
- ☐ Add the sliced onions and sliced mushrooms on top of the potatoes.
- ☐ Sprinkle the diced parsley and grated Parmesan over the onions
- ☐ Cover and bake for 1 hour
- ☐ After one hour, add the frozen peas, cover, and bake for about another 30 minutes.
- ☐ Uncover and let it brown a little bit before taking it out of the oven.

MEATBALLS | *Polpette*

INGREDIENTS

- 1 small onion, chopped
- ½ cup chopped parsley
- 2 large eggs
- 1 tsp garlic powder
- ½ cup grated Parmesan cheese
- 1 lb. ground beef
- ½ cup Italian breadcrumbs
- ¼ cup milk
- Salt and pepper to taste

INSTRUCTIONS

- ☐ Mix all ingredients.
- ☐ Once thoroughly mixed, begin shaping it into small or medium-sized round meatballs, depending on your preference.
- ☐ Place the meatballs on a cookie sheet and freeze them until they are firm.
- ☐ Once the meatballs are partially frozen, transfer them to a Ziplock bag and store them in the freezer until needed.
- ☐ If you need them immediately, don't freeze them; add them directly to the sauce or meal.

42

SAUSAGE CASSEROLE ITALIAN STYLE |
Casseruola di Salsiccia all'Italiana

INGREDIENTS

- 5 Italian sausages or 5 bratwursts (you can mix hot and sweet)
- 8 small potatoes (4 red and 4 Yukon gold), cleaned and sliced in half
- 1 small onion, sliced
- 1 cup frozen peas

- 1 cup of fresh or wild mushrooms, cleaned and cut in half
- 1 cup low-sodium chicken broth
- ½ cup chopped parsley
- ½ tsp Italian seasoning
- ¼ cup grated Parmesan cheese

INSTRUCTIONS

- ☐ 1 medium casserole dish. Preheat oven to 350°F.
- ☐ Spray the bottom of the casserole dish with Pam or olive oil spray.
- ☐ Arrange the sausages on the bottom of the dish.
- ☐ Add the potatoes, mushrooms, and onions.
- ☐ Pour the chicken broth over the ingredients.
- ☐ Sprinkle with parsley, Italian seasoning, and Parmesan cheese.
- ☐ Drizzle olive oil on top before covering.
- ☐ Place in the oven and cook for 40 minutes.
- ☐ Uncover and slowly stir the mixture.
- ☐ Add the peas, then cover and cook for an additional 15 minutes.
- ☐ Uncover and let it cook without a cover for another 10 minutes or until the top is nice and golden.
- ☐ Take it out of the oven, let it sit for about a minute, and then serve.

STEAK PIZZAIOLA | Filetto di Manzo Pizzaiola

INGREDIENTS

- 2 nice pieces of chopped sirloin steak
- 1 (4 oz.) can of mushrooms
- 1 (14 oz.) can of tomato sauce
- 1 (14 oz.) can of petite diced tomatoes w/garlic and oregano
- 1 (4 oz.) can of mushrooms
- 3 cloves of garlic, chopped
- 1 cup mozzarella
- ¼ dry oregano
- ¼ cup chicken broth (low sodium)
- ¼ cup olive oil

INSTRUCTIONS

- ☐ In a blender, blend the two cans of tomatoes and the broth. Set aside.
- ☐ Heat the oil in a medium-sized sauté pan.
- ☐ Once heated, add the garlic, mushrooms, and sauté for about 5 minutes.
- ☐ Add the blended tomatoes and oregano let them slow cook for about 10 minutes.
- ☐ Add the steaks, cover, and cook for 10 to 14 minutes, flipping the steaks several times to cook evenly.
- ☐ Place the mozzarella on top of each piece of steak. Cover and slow cook for 3-5 minutes.
- ☐ Serve individually or over rice or spaghetti.

MARINARA SAUCE

INGREDIENTS

- 1 (28 oz.) can of whole tomatoes (San Marzano preferred)
- 1 small onion, sliced
- ¼ cup extra virgin olive oil
- 3-4 basil leaves, cut in half
- Salt and pepper, to taste

INSTRUCTIONS

- [ ] Place the whole tomatoes in a blender and blend until nice and smooth. Set aside.
- [ ] Heat the olive oil in a small cooking pot.
- [ ] Add the sliced onion and cook until the onion is translucent.
- [ ] Add the blended tomatoes and basil leaves.
- [ ] Simmer for 1 hour.
- [ ] Season with salt and pepper to taste.

45

EASTER PIE | *Pizza Chiena*

INGREDIENTS

Dough

- 4 cups sifted unbleached all-purpose flour (we prefer King Arthur brand)
- 1 tbsp baking powder
- 3 tbsp vegetable shortening, chilled
- 1 tbsp butter, chilled
- 4 large eggs
- ½ cup plus 2 tbsp water
- 1 egg yolk (mixed)
- Pinch of salt

INSTRUCTIONS

- ☐ Whisk together the flour, baking powder, and salt in a large bowl.
- ☐ Using a pastry cutter, cut in the shortening and butter until combined.
- ☐ Make a well in the center of the flour mixture and add the eggs.
- ☐ Stir until just combined.
- ☐ Slowly stir in the water until a dough begins to form.
- ☐ Turn the dough out onto a work surface and knead until the dough is nice and smooth.
- ☐ Form the dough into 2 balls, one slightly larger than the other.
- ☐ Wrap each ball with plastic wrap.
- ☐ Let the dough stand for at least 20 minutes before rolling it out.

- ☐ Roll out the larger ball into a ⅛-inch-thick sheet, approximately 19 by 15 inches.
- ☐ Fit the rolled-out dough into a greased 13x4 inch baking dish, leaving a 1-inch overhang. Set it aside for further use.
- ☐ Preheat oven 375°F

INGREDIENTS

Filling

- 3 ½ lbs. whole milk ricotta
- 18 eggs
- 2 lbs. fresh cheese (1 basket; recipe on page 103)
- 1 cup Parmesan cheese
- ½ lb. soppressata
- ½ lb. capicola
- ½ lb. prosciutto
- ½ lb. Italian salami

46

INSTRUCTIONS

- [ ] Place the ricotta in a large bowl.
- [ ] Add the eggs and mix well.
- [ ] Add Parmesan cheese and mix well.
- [ ] Spoon a part of the mixture into the layered baking dish that has the dough, filling the bottom layer.
- [ ] Layer soppressata and capicola until covered.
- [ ] Spoon more mixture over the top until covered.
- [ ] Layer sliced fresh cheese until covered.
- [ ] Layer prosciutto and Italian salami until covered.
- [ ] Spoon the rest of the mixture over until covered.
- [ ] Add the rest of the sliced fresh cheese.
- [ ] Roll out the smaller dough ball to approximately 14 to 15 inches in diameter.
- [ ] Place the dough over the pie and press down on the edges with a fork.
- [ ] Brush egg yolk over the top.
- [ ] Place the pie in the middle rack of the oven and bake for 3 to 3 ½ hours, checking about every half hour.
- [ ] If the sides begin to cook more, place tin foil around the edges to prevent burning.
- [ ] The pie is done when it turns golden brown, and you can pierce it with a knife, and the knife comes out dry.
- [ ] Once it is cooled, take it out of the baking dish and place it on a platter, being careful not to break it.
- [ ] Let it cool completely before serving.
- [ ] Refrigerate leftovers or freeze them for later.

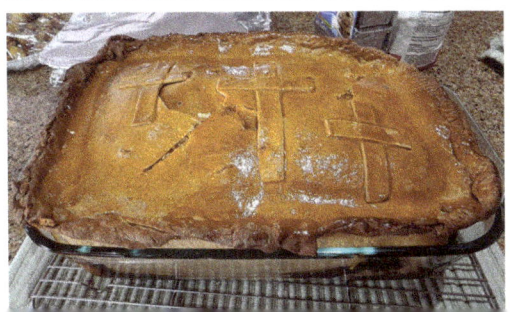

POLLO MARSALA

INGREDIENTS

- 3 tbsp extra virgin olive oil
- 4 boneless chicken breasts, cut lengthwise, pounded to ¼-inch thickness
- 2 cups sliced mushrooms
- ½ cup flour (add more if needed)
- 1 cup Marsala wine
- 1 cup chicken broth
- 2 tbsp butter
- 2 cloves of garlic, chopped
- Salt and pepper, to taste

INSTRUCTIONS

THIS RECIPE SERVES 8

- ☐ In a bowl, mix flour, salt, and pepper.
- ☐ Dip the chicken breasts in flour and set them aside.
- ☐ In a skillet, add olive oil and garlic. Cook until the garlic is golden in color. Remove the garlic and set it aside.
- ☐ Add the floured chicken to the skillet and cook until it reaches a nice golden color. Remove the chicken and set it aside.
- ☐ In the same skillet, add the sliced mushrooms. Add more oil if needed. Stir the mushrooms until they are done.
- ☐ Pour the chicken broth and Marsala wine into the mushrooms in the skillet. Cook until the juice is reduced, about 5-10 minutes.
- ☐ Add the cooked chicken and the garlic back to the skillet. Mix well and cook for an additional 3-5 minutes.
- ☐ Add the butter and stir until melted.
- ☐ Cook for another 2-3 minutes, then transfer the dish to a serving dish.
- ☐ Serve hot.
- ☐ Serve with Italian-crusted bread. A side of spaghetti or other pasta can also be served with it.

CHICKEN PARMESAN | *Pollo Parmigiana*

INGREDIENTS

- Marinara or Ragu sauce (recipe on page 45)
- 2 large chicken breasts
- 4 eggs
- 1 package mozzarella or ½ lb. sliced mozzarella from the deli
- ¼ cup milk

- ½ cup Parmesan cheese (broken down into two ¼ cups)
- 1 ½ cups Italian breadcrumbs
- ¼ cup chopped parsley
- ¼ cup garlic powder
- ½ cup extra virgin olive oil or canola oil
- Salt and pepper, to taste

INSTRUCTIONS

THIS RECIPE SERVES 6

- ☐ Preheat oven to 350°F
- ☐ Fillet the chicken into 3-4 slices, depending on thickness. Pound and set them aside.
- ☐ Whisk the eggs, add milk, ¼ cup Parmesan cheese, and chopped parsley in a bowl. Whisk until nicely blended . Set this mixture aside.
- ☐ Mix breadcrumbs, garlic powder, and ¼ cup Parmesan cheese in another bowl. Mix well.
- ☐ Dip the chicken in the egg mixture and then in the breadcrumb mixture.
- ☐ Preheat oil in a large skillet over medium heat.
- ☐ Gently add the chicken and cook for 2-3 minutes per side until golden brown.
- ☐ Place the cooked chicken on a plate lined with paper towels.
- ☐ Cook all the chicken and place them on a plate.
- ☐ In a large baking dish, layer the bottom with mozzarella.
- ☐ Then, layer sauce on top of the mozzarella.
- ☐ Place the chicken on top of the sauce.
- ☐ Add some more sauce on top.
- ☐ Sprinkle mozzarella on top of the chicken.
- ☐ Cover with tin foil and place it in the oven.
- ☐ Bake the chicken at 350°F for 30 minutes or until it is bubbling and soft when you place a fork in one of the fillets.
- ☐ When done, remove the dish from the oven and serve hot.

PORK BRACIOLA | *Braciola di Maiale*

INGREDIENTS

- 1 ½ - 2 lbs. pork tenderloin (butterflied and slightly pounded), or you can also use pork bellies
- 2 eggs
- 1 cup breadcrumbs (you can also use fresh bread that has been broken up into small pieces)
- ¼ cup Parmesan cheese
- ½ tsp pepper flakes (optional)
- ½ tsp salt
- ¼ cup olive oil
- ¼ cup pine nuts
- ½ cup diced parsley
- 2 tbsp chopped mint

INSTRUCTIONS

- ☐ Mix the breadcrumbs, Parmesan cheese, pepper flakes, pine nuts, parsley, and mint in a small bowl.
- ☐ Add the two eggs and mix thoroughly until the mixture becomes nice and sticky.
- ☐ Lay the tenderloins on a board and flatten them nicely.
- ☐ Evenly spread the breadcrumb mixture on the tenderloins.
- ☐ Roll the tenderloins and tie them with kitchen twine.
- ☐ Heat a medium-sized skillet with the olive oil.
- ☐ Sear the pork tenderloin until it is evenly browned.
- ☐ Add the browned tenderloin to your marinara or meat sauce (recipes on pages 45 and 84).
- ☐ Cover and let it cook until it becomes nice and tender.
- ☐ Remove from heat and let it sit for about 10 minutes before slicing.

You can use either sauce to cook the Braciola. The Italian tradition is that it cooks in the ragu with the other meat and then serve with your favorite pasta.

PORK CHOPS & VINEGAR PEPPERS |
Braciole di maiale e peperoni all'aceto

INGREDIENTS

- 4 bone-in pork chops (medium thickness) or 4 boneless chops (1-inch thick)
- 1 (28 oz.) can San Marzano whole peeled tomatoes (processed in a blender)
- 1 (4 oz.) can of mushrooms or 1 lb. fresh mushrooms (cleaned and sliced)
- 1 (16 oz.) jar of Mezzetta Sweet Cherry Peppers
- 3 large garlic cloves
- ¼ cup olive oil
- Salt and ground black pepper

INSTRUCTIONS

- ☐ Clean the vinegar peppers but save half of the juice.
- ☐ Slice the peppers in half and set them aside.
- ☐ Heat oil in a large skillet over medium heat.
- ☐ When hot, pat the chops dry, sprinkle with salt and ground pepper on both sides and add them to the skillet.
- ☐ Lower the heat and cook for 5-8 minutes until they become nice and golden.
- ☐ Remove the chops from the skillet, set them aside on a plate, and keep them warm.
- ☐ Add the garlic, mushrooms, and peppers (along with part of the juice) to the skillet.
- ☐ Cook for 3-4 minutes, stirring until the peppers are heated through.
- ☐ Place the chops back in the skillet, and add the tomatoes and the rest of the pepper juice.
- ☐ Stir to cover the chops nicely, then cover the skillet and slow cook for 2-3 hours until the chops are nice and tender.
- ☐ Add red pepper flakes if desired.
- ☐ Serve with crusty bread. It can also be served over rice.

SAUSAGE AND PEPPERS | *Salciccia e Pepperoni*

INGREDIENTS

- 6 sweet Italian sausages
- 6 mild or hot Italian sausages
- 1 lb. baby bella mushrooms or white mushrooms, cleaned and sliced
- 1 medium-sized onion, sliced
- 2 large bell peppers, your choice of colors
- 3 cloves of garlic, diced
- 1 tbsp garlic powder
- ¼ cup olive oil

INSTRUCTIONS

- ☐ In a medium skillet, heat the oil.
- ☐ Sauté the sausages until they become nice and golden brown. Take them out and set them aside. (You can either slice the sausages or leave them whole)
- ☐ Add the peppers, onion, garlic, and mushrooms to the oil.
- ☐ Sauté everything for about 10 to 15 minutes.
- ☐ Add the mushrooms and sausages back into the mixture and cook until the peppers and onions are nice and tender.
- ☐ Serve hot on a hoagie roll or as a side with rice or pasta.

Tip: You can also add meatballs to this dish. Sauté the meatballs with the sausages.

PASTA

Pasta

CAVATELLI

INGREDIENTS

- 3 cups of unbleached all-purpose flour (or semolina, if available)
- 1 cup of warm water
- ½ tsp salt

INSTRUCTIONS

- ☐ Place the flour on a clean work surface. Make a well in the center of the flour and sprinkle in the salt.
- ☐ Pour ½ cup of water into the well you've made in the flour.
- ☐ Begin combining the water and flour using your fingers. Gradually add the remaining water while continuously mixing. If you need, add a little water in small increments. The goal is to achieve a soft and workable dough.
- ☐ Knead the dough vigorously for 5-10 minutes and shape it into a ball.
- ☐ Wrap the dough ball with a clean dish towel or plastic wrap and let it rest for about 30 minutes.
- ☐ Take ¼ of the dough and shape it into a sausage-like form.
- ☐ Roll out the dough into a long rope approximately ½-inch thick. If the dough becomes sticky, lightly dust your work surface with flour as needed.
- ☐ If the rope becomes too long, cut it in half. Then, cut the rope into pieces measuring ¾ to 1-inch each.
- ☐ Using your index and middle fingers, firmly press onto each piece of dough and drag it towards you, creating a curled shape and an indentation.
- ☐ Place the prepared pasta pieces in a single layer on a cookie sheet dusted with flour or lined with parchment paper. Ensure that the pieces do not touch each other.
- ☐ Once the cookie sheet is filled, place it in the freezer.
- ☐ Repeat the process with the remaining dough.
- ☐ After a couple of hours in the freezer, transfer the pasta to a zip-lock bag and return it to the freezer. Keep it frozen until you're ready to cook it. However, if you plan to cook the pasta on the same day, there's no need to freeze it.
- ☐ In a large pot, bring salted water to a boil.
- ☐ Once the water is boiling, add the frozen or unfrozen pasta and cook for 8-10 minutes. Be cautious not to overcook, which can result in overly soft pasta.
- ☐ Serve with your favorite sauce.

FETTUCCINI ALFREDO

INGREDIENTS

- 1 (16 oz.) bottle of whipping cream
- 1 stick of butter
- 1 lb. fresh fettuccini (found in the refrigerator section of the grocery store)
- 1 ½ cups Parmesan cheese
- Red pepper flakes (optional)
- ¼ cup fresh chopped parsley (optional)

INSTRUCTIONS

- ☐ Begin by filling a medium-sized pot with water and boiling it.
- ☐ Add the fresh fettuccini to the boiling water and cook according to the directions provided on the package.
- ☐ Meanwhile, in a large skillet or pan, melt the butter over medium heat.
- ☐ Stir in 1 ½ cups of whipping cream and allow the cream to reduce for approximately 5 minutes.
- ☐ Add half of the Parmesan cheese to the cream mixture. Stir the sauce until it becomes smooth and the cheese is fully melted.
- ☐ Save some pasta water, as it can be useful for thinning the sauce if needed.
- ☐ Toss the fettuccini directly in the prepared Alfredo sauce.
- ☐ Add the remaining Parmesan cheese to the fettuccini and sauce mixture and toss thoroughly.
- ☐ Transfer the dish to a serving platter and sprinkle with parsley.

DITALINI AND CAULIFLOWER | *Ditalini e Cavolfiore*

INGREDIENTS

- 1 (28 oz.) can of Cento diced tomatoes in garlic, oregano, and basil (dice in blender).
- 1 small or medium cauliflower, cleaned and cut into stems

- 1 medium garlic, sliced into medium pieces
- ¼ cup olive oil
- 2 basil leaves

INSTRUCTIONS

- ☐ In a small pan, add 8 cups of water and bring it to a boil. Place the cut and cleaned cauliflower in the boiling water. Simmer for about 10 minutes until almost tender. You only want to blanch the cauliflower as it will cook in the sauce.

- ☐ In a medium skillet, heat the olive oil.

- ☐ Add the onion and cook until it turns a nice golden color.

- ☐ Add the diced tomatoes and basil and cook for about 20 minutes until everything is nicely blended.

- ☐ Add the blanched cauliflower, cover, and cook on low heat for about 20 minutes or until the cauliflower is nice and tender (but not soft).

- ☐ Serve with Parmesan cheese and crusty bread, or enjoy it as a side dish.

LASAGNA

INGREDIENTS

- 1 lb. package of lasagna pasta (cooked per directions and set aside)
- 2 lbs. whole milk ricotta
- 1 cup Parmesan cheese
- ½ cup fresh parsley (chopped)
- 4 eggs
- 1 lb. mozzarella cheese
- Ragu sauce (recipe on page 45)

INSTRUCTIONS

Serves 8

- ☐ 10x12 by 2-inch deep baking pan
- ☐ Heat oven to 375°F
- ☐ Place the ricotta in a large bowl.
- ☐ Add the eggs and mix until nicely blended.
- ☐ Add parsley and Parmesan cheese.
- ☐ When smooth, start layering the lasagna pan.
- ☐ Spray the bottom of the pan with Pam.

- ☐ Cover the bottom of the pan with ragu sauce.
- ☐ Add the lasagna noodles to cover the bottom.
- ☐ Spread the ricotta mixture over the noodles until they are nicely covered.
- ☐ Sprinkle mozzarella on top and add Parmesan cheese.
- ☐ Add another layer of ragu sauce.
- ☐ Add another layer of lasagna noodles.
- ☐ Repeat this step 2 more times until the pan is almost filled.
- ☐ Sprinkle the top with more ragu sauce, mozzarella, and Parmesan cheese.
- ☐ Place in the oven and cook for about 45 minutes.
- ☐ Uncover and let it slightly brown on the top for another 10-15 minutes.
- ☐ Take it out of the oven and let it rest for about 30-45 minutes or longer until it looks nice and firm.

Tip: You can use the same recipe for Manicotti and Stuffed Shells. Cook the pasta per the directions on the box and then stuff.

Pictures from top to bottom: Manicotti, stuffed shells, and birds nest.

NANA'S TORTELLINI

INGREDIENTS

- 1 (20 oz.) family size tortellini
- 1 ½ lbs. frozen peas
- 1 large sweet onion, chopped
- 1 tbsp of olive oil
- 1 cup Parmesan cheese

INSTRUCTIONS

- ☐ Place oil in a sauté pan.
- ☐ Add the onion and sauté until it's soft.
- ☐ Add peas, toss with onions, and simmer.
- ☐ Boil water in another pan.
- ☐ Place tortellini in the boiling water and boil for 3 minutes.
- ☐ Using a slotted ladle, strain the pasta and place it in the onion and peas mixture.
- ☐ Add ½ cup of hot water from the pasta. Stir well.
- ☐ Stir in ¾ cup of Parmesan cheese.
- ☐ Mix and place the pasta in a bowl.
- ☐ Sprinkle the remaining Parmesan on top.

BAKED ZITI | *Ziti al Forno*

INGREDIENTS

- 1 lb. Ziti
- 1 (15oz.) container of whole ricotta
- 3 eggs
- ¾ cup Parmesan cheese
- 1 (16 oz.) package of mozzarella cheese
- Sauce: Can be marinara or ragu. Recipe on page 45

INSTRUCTIONS

- ☐ Preheat the oven to 375°F.
- ☐ Cook ziti according to the directions on the box.
- ☐ Mix ricotta, eggs, and 1 oz. of mozzarella cheese in a medium bowl.
- ☐ To cover the bottom, spoon a small amount of sauce into a casserole dish (14x10 inch).
- ☐ Spoon in the cooked ziti into the ricotta mixture. Mix well.
- ☐ Spoon in half of the ziti mixture into the casserole.
- ☐ Add some sauce and mozzarella over the top.
- ☐ Repeat this one more time.
- ☐ Cover and cook for about 40 minutes.
- ☐ Uncover and cook for an additional 10 minutes or until lightly golden on top.

61

NOODLES WITH CHICKPEAS | *Tagliatelle e Ceci*

INGREDIENTS

- 1 small onion, finely chopped
- ½ lb. tagliatelle or fresh-made Italian noodles (recipe on page 63)
- 1 (8 oz.) can of chickpeas or ½ lb. fresh chickpeas (follow instructions for overnight soaking)
- 2 garlic cloves, finely diced
- ½ cup fresh parsley, chopped
- 1 small can of diced tomatoes (chop in blender)
- Hot pepper flakes, if desired
- Salt and pepper, to taste
- Parmesan cheese for topping

INSTRUCTIONS

- ☐ Sauté the onion and garlic in some oil in a medium-sized pan.
- ☐ Add the crushed tomatoes when the onion and garlic are nice and soft.
- ☐ Cook for 4-5 minutes, then add the chickpeas and parsley.
- ☐ Cook for another 4-5 minutes until nice and blended.
- ☐ Cook the noodles in salted water.
- ☐ Add a couple of tablespoons of pasta water to the sauce.
- ☐ Drain the noodles and add them to the chickpea sauce mixture.
- ☐ Toss and serve.

HOMEMADE NOODLES | *Tagliatelle Fatte in Casa*

INGREDIENTS

- ½ lb. semolina flour or unbleached all-purpose flour
- 1 cup of warm water (you might need to add more if needed)

INSTRUCTIONS

- ☐ Place the flour in a bowl and slowly add the water, mixing with a fork until the flour and water begin to come together. Add water as needed; you might have some left over.
- ☐ Once the dough is made, cover it with plastic wrap and let it rest for about an hour.
- ☐ After resting, divide the dough into 4 pieces. Roll out one piece at a time to flatten, then use a pasta machine to bring it to the desired thickness for noodles. Use a rolling pin if you don't have a pasta machine.
- ☐ Once the desired thickness is achieved, run the dough through the pasta machine on the noodle setting, cutting it into noodles.
- ☐ Lay the noodles on a clean kitchen towel and set them aside.

Tip: For egg noodles substitute the water with 2 eggs.

63

PASTA E FAGGIOLI WITH PEPPERONI

INGREDIENTS

- 1 Boar's Head pepperoni stick, sliced
- 1 bag of 15-bean mix (follow the overnight soaking directions on the bag)
- ½ bunch of Italian parsley, cleaned and chopped
- 5 large garlic cloves, diced

- 1 tbsp of olive oil
- 1 cup Ditalini pasta
- 4 (32 oz.) cartons of low-sodium chicken broth
- 1 chicken bouillon cube
- 1 can (8 oz.) of petite diced tomatoes

Optional: Pork ribs can also be added to the recipe. Use country style or half of a pork sparerib.

INSTRUCTIONS

- ☐ Place the chicken broth in a slow cooker.
- ☐ Add the seasoning bag from the beans.
- ☐ Add the sliced pepperoni and ribs (if you are going to add ribs).
- ☐ Add the beans.
- ☐ Add the parsley.
- ☐ Add the diced garlic.
- ☐ Add the olive oil.
- ☐ Add the chopped tomatoes. You can blend them first if you prefer a smoother texture (tomatoes are optional).
- ☐ Cook on low for 6-8 hours or until the beans are tender.
- ☐ Add the Ditalini pasta and cook until al dente.
- ☐ Serve with crusty bread and Parmesan cheese.
- ☐ If needed, add more broth or water along with the bouillon cube.
- ☐ Optional: Add mixed greens about half an hour before it is done—greens like endive, collard greens, mustard greens, kale, or any type you like. Clean the greens, cut them into medium-sized pieces, or break them into the bean mixture. Cook them with the beans for half an hour before they are done. Greens do not take that long to cook.

ZITI AND BROCCOLI

INGREDIENTS

- ¼ cup of extra virgin olive oil
- 1 lb. ziti
- 1 ½ lbs. broccoli (cleaned and broken up into pieces)
- ¼ cup or more Parmesan cheese
- 3 cloves of garlic (sliced into small slices)
- Pinch of salt
- ¼ tsp red pepper flakes (optional)

INSTRUCTIONS

THIS RECIPE SERVES 4

- ☐ In a large pan, bring water to a boil.
- ☐ Place a drop of oil in the water.
- ☐ Bring salted water to a boil in another large pan and add the broccoli spears/florets. Cook until almost done; do not overcook.
- ☐ Drop the 1 lb. of ziti into boiling water and cook according to box instructions. Drain and set aside.
- ☐ In a medium sauté pan, put half of the oil and the sliced garlic. Sauté for about 5 minutes until a nice golden color is achieved.
- ☐ Add the broccoli, cover, and cook until the broccoli is al dente.
- ☐ Add the rest of the cooked ziti and oil. Stir until nicely blended. Cook for about 5 minutes.
- ☐ Add Parmesan cheese before serving.

65

RAVIOLI

INGREDIENTS

RAVIOLI FILLING

- 1 lb. whole milk ricotta (drain liquid)
- 2 eggs
- 1 ½ tsp parsley, chopped
- 1 ½ cups Parmesan cheese

INSTRUCTIONS

- ☐ Mix all of the above ingredients in a bowl.
- ☐ Place the bowl in the refrigerator until the ravioli is ready to be filled.

INGREDIENTS

RAVIOLI DOUGH

- 3 cups of all-purpose flour (unbleached or semolina if you have it)
- 1 cup of warm water
- 2 eggs
- ½ tsp salt

INSTRUCTIONS

- ☐ Mound the flour and salt on a dough board and form a well.
- ☐ Beat the eggs and water in a bowl. Pour half of the egg mixture into the well.
- ☐ Begin mixing the egg and flour with one hand while using your other hand to keep the flour mound steady.
- ☐ Add the remaining egg mixture and knead to form a dough.
- ☐ Keep kneading the dough until it is nice and smooth. Add more flour if the dough is sticky.
- ☐ Form the dough into a ball and wrap it tightly with plastic. Refrigerate for an hour.
- ☐ Roll out the pasta dough into thin sheets, about ⅛-inch thick.
- ☐ To prevent the dough from sticking on the ravioli rack, dust one side of the sheet before placing it on the rack.
- ☐ Place the floured side down on the ravioli rack.

- [ ] Spoon the filling into each hole, pressing a little to get it settled in there.
- [ ] Place another sheet on top of the other sheet that has the filling.
- [ ] Roll a rolling pin over the top sheet, firmly rolling back and forth until the ravioli fall through the rack.
- [ ] Repeat this process until all the dough is finished.

Tip: If you don't have a ravioli rack, drop cheese filling in 1 teaspoon portions onto the dough about 1-inch apart. Cover the filling with the top sheet of pasta. Cut out individual ravioli with the open end of a small round glass, pressing the glass over each ravioli until they are sealed. Alternatively, you can use ravioli cutters.

COOKING INSTRUCTIONS

- [ ] Place a large pot of water on the stove and bring it to a boil.
- [ ] Stir in the ravioli and bring them to a boil.
- [ ] Cook uncovered, stirring occasionally, until the ravioli float to the top (about 4 to 8 minutes).
- [ ] Drain the ravioli well and place them in a serving bowl.
- [ ] Top with your favorite sauce, such as marinara or Ragu (recipe on page 45).

PASTIERE

INGREDIENTS

- **1 lb. whole milk ricotta**
- **3 eggs**
- **½ cup Parmesan cheese**
- **¼ cup diced parsley (optional)**
- **¼ cup milk**
- **½ lb. spaghetti**

INSTRUCTIONS

- ☐ Preheat oven to 375°F.
- ☐ Grease an 11x9 glass baking dish. Set aside
- ☐ Place the ricotta in a large bowl.
- ☐ Add eggs and mix thoroughly.
- ☐ Add Parmesan cheese and mix thoroughly.
- ☐ In a large pot, boil spaghetti until al dente. Drain and rinse in cold water.
- ☐ Add the cooked spaghetti to the bowl with the ricotta mixture. Mix thoroughly.
- ☐ Place the mixture in the greased baking dish.
- ☐ Add small pats of butter to the top, then cover with tin foil and bake for 1 hour.
- ☐ Unwrap and bake for an additional 20 minutes until the top is golden brown.
- ☐ You can eat it hot or wait for it to cool down completely. It makes great leftovers; just reheat and serve.
- ☐ Red pepper flakes are optional to sprinkle on top of the slices.

SEAFOOD
Frutti di Mare

BAKED COD | *Merluzzo al forno*

INGREDIENTS

- 8 medium (3 lbs.) cod filets
- 4 cloves of garlic, chopped
- 1 cup parsley, chopped
- ¾ cup Parmesan cheese
- 3 cups fresh Italian bread (cut or broken into small pieces)
- ¼ cup olive oil
- 1 tsp ground pepper

INSTRUCTIONS

- ☐ Heat oven to 375°F.
- ☐ Place the cod filets in a baking dish sprayed with Pam.
- ☐ Combine the bread, garlic, parsley, Parmesan cheese, and ground pepper in a bowl.
- ☐ Add oil to bread mixture and mix until moist.
- ☐ Spread the mixed ingredients evenly over the cod.
- ☐ Drizzle olive oil over the top.
- ☐ Cover with tin foil and bake for 30 minutes.
- ☐ Uncover and bake for another 10-15 minutes until it's golden and crunchy on top.
- ☐ Serve immediately.

STUFFED SHRIMP | *Gamberi ripieni*

INGREDIENTS

- 1 lb. raw extra-large shrimp or prawns
- 2 cups Italian breadcrumbs
- 1 cup Parmesan cheese
- ½ cup chopped parsley
- ¼ cup chopped garlic
- Olive oil
- ¼ tsp of ground pepper

INSTRUCTIONS

- ☐ Heat oven to 375°F.
- ☐ Clean and devein shrimp.
- ☐ Butterfly cut them and place them in a baking pan sprayed with Pam.
- ☐ Mix breadcrumbs, Parmesan cheese, parsley, garlic, and ground pepper in a bowl.
- ☐ Add olive oil a little at a time until the mixture becomes like a paste.
- ☐ Place the mixture on each individual shrimp until all shrimp are coated.
- ☐ Drizzle some olive oil over the top.
- ☐ Cover the pan and place it in the oven.
- ☐ Cook for 20 minutes or longer, depending on the oven.
- ☐ Uncover and continue to cook.
- ☐ The shrimp is done when the stuffing is nice and golden brown.

CIOPPINO

INGREDIENTS

- ¼ cup butter
- ¼ cup oil
- 2 onions, chopped
- 2 cloves of garlic, minced
- 1 cup chopped Italian parsley
- 1 (32 oz.) can of Cento plum tomatoes in a thick sauce
- 1 (16 oz.) can of low-sodium chicken broth
- 2 bay leaves
- ¼ cup chopped fresh basil
- 1 tsp dried thyme
- 1 tsp dried oregano
- 1 pinch of dry fennel
- 1 tsp Italian dry seasoning mix
- 1 cup white wine
- 1 small can of tomato paste (if you want a thicker broth)
- Seafood
- 1 lb. large shrimp, peeled and deveined
- 1 lb. bay scallops
- 1 dozen small clams, scrubbed and cleaned
- 1 dozen mussels, cleaned

Other seafood that can be used: ½ lb. lobster claws, 1 lb. crabmeat, 1 lb. cod fillets (cubed), 1 lb. calamari rings. Any other seafood that you like can be part of this dish.

INSTRUCTIONS

- ☐ In a nice-sized stock pot, heat the oil.
- ☐ Add onions, garlic, and parsley. Cook until the onion is nice and soft.
- ☐ Add the tomatoes and chicken broth.
- ☐ Add the bay leaves, oregano, basil, thyme, and wine. Mix well.
- ☐ Cover and simmer for 1 hour.
- ☐ Add the butter and stir until well mixed, then let it simmer for 10 more minutes.
- ☐ Add the seafood, cover, and simmer for about 10 minutes or until the clams open up.
- ☐ Ladle the mixture into soup bowls and add crusted bread for dipping.
- ☐ Before serving, make sure you remove the bay leaves.
- ☐ Optional: If desired, cook ½ lb. of spaghetti according to the box instructions. Ladle the seafood mixture over the spaghetti and serve.

COD SALAD | *Baccala Insalata*

INGREDIENTS

- 8 cod fillets (frozen is okay)
- 1 large green pepper, sliced
- 3 garlic cloves, diced
- ½ cup fresh parsley, sliced
- ½ lb. dry oil-cured Italian olives
- 2 stalks of celery, sliced
- ¼ cup extra-virgin olive oil
- Salt and pepper, to taste

INSTRUCTIONS

- ☐ In a large pan, bring the cod fillets to a boil. Simmer and cook until tender. Don't overcook.
- ☐ Drain the cod fillets and run cold water over them. Set them aside and let them cool.
- ☐ Once the cod is nice and cool, break it up into bite-size pieces and place them in a bowl.
- ☐ Add the sliced peppers, diced garlic, parsley, and sliced celery to the bowl.
- ☐ Add the olives to the mixture.
- ☐ Pour in the olive oil.
- ☐ Toss the ingredients together and place the bowl in the refrigerator until you're ready to serve.

CLAMS CASINO | *Vongole al Casino*

INGREDIENTS

- 12 hard shell clams (littlenecks or cherrystones), scrubbed
- ½ cup Italian-style breadcrumbs

- ¼ cup finely chopped parsley
- 3 slices of bacon, sliced crosswise
- 1 fresh lemon

INSTRUCTIONS

- ☐ Preheat the oven to 350°F.
- ☐ Shuck the clams and discard the top shell.
- ☐ Place the clams on a baking sheet
- ☐ Sprinkle bread crumbs over each clam.
- ☐ Add the sliced bacon on top.
- ☐ Squeeze a little bit of lemon juice over each clam.
- ☐ Bake until the bacon is nice and crispy.
- ☐ Serve hot.
- ☐ Optional: You can enhance the topping by adding finely sliced green or red pepper.

Tip: If fresh clams are unavailable, you can substitute canned clams. You'll need small ramekins for baking. Place a teaspoon of clams in each ramekin and follow the rest of the recipe as above.

SPAGHETTI & CLAMS | Spaghetti e' Vongole

INGREDIENTS

- 1 can of chopped clams
- ½ cup of fresh parsley, diced
- 3 garlic cloves, diced

- ½ lb. of spaghetti or fettuccini
- ½ cup olive oil
- ½ stick of butter

INSTRUCTIONS

- ☐ Place half of the olive oil in a skillet.
- ☐ Drain the clams and add them to the oil. Cook for about 10 minutes.
- ☐ Add the garlic and cook for about 5 minutes.
- ☐ Add the parsley, butter, and the rest of the olive oil. Cook for about 5 minutes.
- ☐ While cooking the clams, prepare the spaghetti or fettuccine in a large pan according to the instructions on the box. Drain well and place in a large serving bowl.
- ☐ Add the clam sauce to the pasta in the serving bowl and stir well.
- ☐ Top with Parmesan cheese and red pepper flakes.
- ☐ Optional: You can add the cooked pasta directly to the skillet with the clam sauce instead of transferring it to a separate bowl.

76

SCALLOPS | *Scaloppine*

INGREDIENTS

- 1 ½ lbs. nice-sized sea scallops
- 1 tbsp butter
- 1 tbsp extra virgin olive oil
- 1 lemon
- 3 garlic cloves
- ¼ cup low-sodium chicken broth
- ¼ cup white wine
- Salt and pepper

INSTRUCTIONS

- ☐ Pat the scallops thoroughly dry with paper towels and season them with salt and pepper.
- ☐ Heat a skillet over high heat, then add the oil and butter.
- ☐ Once the oil and butter are hot, add the scallops to the skillet, ensuring they are spaced apart so they do not touch.
- ☐ Cook the scallops for 2 minutes without disturbing them, allowing a nice golden crust to form on the bottom.
- ☐ Gently reduce the heat to medium-high, flip the scallops to the other side, and cook for an additional 1-2 minutes until golden on the bottom.
- ☐ Keep a close eye on the scallops to prevent overcooking, as they usually cook quickly.
- ☐ Remove the scallops from the pan and place them on a serving plate. Serve them hot.
- ☐ Serve the scallops with a garlic butter sauce, or enjoy them as they are.

GARLIC BUTTER SAUCE

- ☐ In the same skillet that the scallops were cooked in, add 2 tbsp of butter.
- ☐ Add 3-4 cloves of garlic, juice from half a lemon, ¼ cup white wine, and ¼ cup of low-sodium chicken broth.
- ☐ Cook the sauce for 2 minutes.
- ☐ Serve the garlic butter sauce over the scallops and garnish with chopped parsley.

STEAMED MUSSELS AND CLAMS | *Cozze e Vongole al Vapore*

INGREDIENTS

- 3-4 lbs. baby clams
- 3-4 lbs. fresh mussels
- 3 large garlic cloves, sliced
- ½ cup diced parsley

- ¼ cup extra virgin olive oil
- 3 cups white wine (more if it doesn't seem like enough)

INSTRUCTIONS

- ☐ Prepare the mussels and clams by washing them thoroughly.
- ☐ Place the clams and mussels in a large skillet.
- ☐ Pour in the wine and olive oil.
- ☐ Sprinkle the parsley and sliced garlic on top.
- ☐ Cover the skillet and shake it gently to mix all the ingredients.
- ☐ Steam the clams and mussels until they open up.
- ☐ Scoop out the clams and mussels and place them in a serving dish.
- ☐ Put the remaining liquid in a couple of small bowls, making sure not to pour all of it in, in case sand residue is at the bottom. This liquid is used to rinse the mussels or clams before eating.
- ☐ Serve the clams and mussels with small bowls of melted butter on the side.

SHRIMP SCAMPI

INGREDIENTS

- 1 lb. raw shrimp (large or extra-large), cleaned and deveined
- 2 tbsp butter
- 2 tbsp extra virgin olive oil
- 4 garlic cloves, minced
- ½ cup white wine
- 1 tsp crushed red pepper (optional)
- ¼ cup chopped parsley
- Salt and pepper, to taste

INSTRUCTIONS

- ☐ Place the cleaned shrimp in a container with a lid.
- ☐ Add minced garlic, lemon juice, a drop of olive oil, and half of the chopped parsley to the container. Toss the mixture to coat the shrimp. Cover the container and refrigerate for a couple of hours or at least one hour to marinate.
- ☐ Heat the remaining olive oil in a wok or sauté pan.
- ☐ Once heated, add the marinated shrimp to the wok or pan, tossing them while cooking.
- ☐ Pour in the white wine and add the rest of the chopped parsley.
- ☐ Squeeze in a little more lemon juice and add red pepper flakes if desired.
- ☐ Allow the wine to reduce by half, ensuring the shrimp are cooked until they turn a nice pink color.
- ☐ Serve the cooked shrimp over linguini, spaghetti, or crostini bread (sliced French bread that has been toasted).

SOUPS AND SAUCES

Zuppe e Salsei

ITALIAN WEDDING SOUP | *Zuppa Matrimoniale*

INGREDIENTS

- 3 (32 oz.) low-sodium chicken broth
- 1 beef bouillon cube
- 1 lb. of endive or escarole, chopped into medium-sized pieces
- ¾ cup diced onion
- ½ cup diced parsley
- 2 eggs

- ½ cup of Acini di Pepe pasta (or substitute with mini shells or tubetini if Acini di Pepe pasta is unavailable)
- ¼ cup Parmesan cheese
- Meatball recipe on page 85

INSTRUCTIONS

- ☐ In a large pot, bring the chicken broth, beef cube, diced onion, and parsley to a boil over medium-high heat. Cook for about 10 minutes.

- ☐ Add the meatballs and curly endive, then simmer until the meatballs are fully cooked and the curly endive is tender, approximately 15 minutes. Stir in the pasta and continue cooking for an additional 10 minutes.

- ☐ Whisk the eggs and Parmesan cheese together in a medium bowl until well blended.

- ☐ Stir the soup in a circular motion. Gradually drizzle the egg mixture into the moving broth while stirring gently with a fork to create thin strands of egg, about 1 minute.

- ☐ Season the soup with salt and pepper. Be cautious with salt due to the potential saltiness of the cheese. Add pepper, then taste and determine if additional salt is needed.

- ☐ When serving, drizzle fresh Parmesan cheese on top.

CHICKEN SOUP | *Zuppa di Pollo*

INGREDIENTS

- 3 chicken legs and 3 chicken thighs (boneless chicken breasts can be used as an alternative)
- 1 bunch of Italian parsley, cleaned and diced
- 2 large onions, sliced
- 4 large carrots, sliced
- 4 large stalks of celery, sliced
- 3 (32 oz.) low-sodium chicken broth
- 3 cups frozen peas
- 1 or 2 chicken bouillon cubes

INSTRUCTIONS

- ☐ In a large stock pot, combine the chicken broth and chicken pieces.
- ☐ Cook over medium heat for about 2 hours or until the chicken is fully cooked.
- ☐ Remove the chicken from the pot and place it in a bowl. Allow it to cool.
- ☐ While the chicken is cooling, add the diced Italian parsley, sliced onions, sliced carrots, and sliced celery to the simmering stock. Bring the mixture to a boil, reduce the heat, and let it simmer.
- ☐ Clean the cooled chicken while the vegetables are cooking and cut it into strips or small slices.
- ☐ Place the chicken pieces back into the pot with the vegetables and broth.
- ☐ The soup is ready when the vegetables reach the desired level of tenderness. Be careful not to overcook.

MINESTRONE SOUP

INGREDIENTS

- 2 large sweet onions, chopped
- 2 cloves of garlic, diced
- 1 cup garbanzo beans, soaked overnight per instructions on the bag
- 1 cup Northern white beans, soaked overnight per instructions on the bag
- 1 cup chopped parsley
- 1 ½ cups chopped carrots
- 4 stalks of celery, chopped
- 2 cups string beans, cleaned and cut into small slices
- 3 zucchini, sliced

- 1 cup frozen peas
- 1 bunch of endive or escarole or any type of greens you prefer, cut into small pieces
- ¼ cup extra virgin olive oil
- 1 (32 oz.) can low-sodium chicken broth
- 1 (28 oz.) can Cento tomatoes, whole or chopped
- 2 bay leaves
- 2 tbsp Italian seasoning
- Ground pepper
- Ditalini pasta (Optional)

INSTRUCTIONS

- [ ] In a large stock pot, heat the olive oil.
- [ ] Sauté the chopped onion and diced garlic.
- [ ] Add the chopped carrots.
- [ ] Stir in the chopped celery.
- [ ] Add the Cento tomatoes to the pot.
- [ ] Mix in the chopped parsley.
- [ ] Pour in the low-sodium chicken broth.
- [ ] Allow the mixture to cook for about 10 minutes.
- [ ] Incorporate the sliced string beans, soaked garbanzo beans, and soaked Northern white beans into the pot.

- [ ] Add the bay leaves, Italian seasoning, and ground pepper.
- [ ] Cover the pot and cook for approximately 20 minutes.
- [ ] Introduce the sliced zucchini and your choice of greens to the mixture.
- [ ] Cover the pot once more and continue cooking until fully cooked.
- [ ] Stir occasionally. Soup is done when all ingredients are tender.
- [ ] Remove bay leaves before serving.
- [ ] Optional, add ditalini pasta. Cook the pasta separately then add it to the soup.

NANA'S PASTA SAUCE – RAGU | *Il Ragu Della Nonna*

INGREDIENTS

- 10 meatballs (recipe on page 85)
- 1 28 oz. can of crushed tomatoes in puree
- 1 (12 oz.) can of tomato paste
- 1 (15 oz.) can of tomato sauce
- 1 (15 oz.) can of tomato puree
- 1 sweet onion, chopped

- 10 fresh basil leaves cut in half
- 1 cup of red wine
- Extra virgin olive oil
- 3 or 4 country-style pork spare ribs
- 3 or 4 links of Italian sausage
- Salt and pepper to taste

INSTRUCTIONS

- ☐ In a large nonstick pot, add about a tablespoon of oil.
- ☐ Prick the sausages with a fork.
- ☐ Place the sausages and pork ribs in the pan and cook until golden brown on all sides.
- ☐ Add the chopped onion. Allow it to cook until the onion becomes translucent.
- ☐ Pour in about a cup of red wine (you can experiment with the amount as you go along).
- ☐ Stir the meat so that all sides are flavored with the wine. Allow the wine to evaporate.
- ☐ Incorporate the can of tomato paste and let it cook for a while.
- ☐ Fill the tomato paste can with water and pour it into the pot.
- ☐ Add the crushed tomatoes, tomato sauce, and tomato puree to the pot. Stir and mix well.
- ☐ Add the fresh basil and let it simmer for a few minutes.
- ☐ Add the meatballs (recipe on following page).
- ☐ Allow the sauce to simmer, covered for 2 hours or more. Longer cooking time results in better flavor, but a minimum of 2 hours is necessary.
- ☐ Stir occasionally.

NANA'S MEATBALLS

INGREDIENTS

- 1 lb. ground beef (93% lean)
- 1 egg
- ½ cup fresh of chopped parsley
- ½ cup of Italian-style breadcrumbs
- 1 tsp of garlic powder
- ½ cup of grated Parmesan cheese
- ¼ cup of milk
- Salt and pepper, to taste

INSTRUCTIONS

SERVES AT LEAST FOUR PEOPLE

- ☐ Combine ground beef, parsley, egg, breadcrumbs, garlic powder, grated Parmesan cheese, salt, pepper, and milk in a large bowl.
- ☐ Thoroughly mix all the ingredients and shape them into small balls.
- ☐ Add the meatballs to the sauce and let everything cook for 2 hours or more.

Tip: You can make the meatballs fresh while making the sauce once the sauce has started to simmer. Alternatively, to save time, you can prepare the meatballs ahead of time and freeze them. They can be added to the simmering sauce directly from the freezer and cooked with the rest of the meat.

85

VEGETABLES

Verdura

EGGPLANT PARMIGIANA | *Melanzane parmigiana*

INGREDIENTS

- 2 medium eggplants, washed and cut into ½-inch thick rounds
- 5 large eggs
- 3 tbsp milk
- 4 cups Italian breadcrumbs
- ¼ cup freshly chopped parsley

- Olive oil for frying, as needed
- ½ cup Parmesan cheese
- 1 large bag of mozzarella or a whole mozzarella, cut into slices
- Sauce: Marinara or Ragu sauce (Recipes on page 45 or 84)

INSTRUCTIONS

- ☐ Preheat the oven to 350°F.
- ☐ Place about ½ cup of oil in a frying pan and heat it.
- ☐ Combine breadcrumbs and Parmesan cheese in a bowl.
- ☐ Beat the 5 eggs in another bowl. Add parsley and milk, and beat until well blended.
- ☐ Dip the eggplant slices in the egg batter, then coat them in the breadcrumb mixture, making sure they're well coated on both sides.
- ☐ Place each coated eggplant slice in the hot oil. Turn them over when one side is nicely browned, then cook the other side. Remove and place on a baking pan lined with paper towels to absorb excess oil. Repeat until all eggplant slices are cooked.
- ☐ In a 9x13 inch baking dish, spread a layer of sauce on the bottom.
- ☐ Top with a layer of fried eggplant slices.
- ☐ Add a layer of mozzarella on top of the eggplant.
- ☐ Spoon sauce over the mozzarella.
- ☐ Repeat the layering process until all the eggplant is used, creating about 3 layers.
- ☐ Finish with a layer of remaining mozzarella and some sauce.
- ☐ Place the baking dish in the oven and cook until the cheese is melted and bubbly, about 40 minutes.
- ☐ Once done, remove it from the oven and let it sit for about 15 minutes before serving

Refer to the separate Marinara or Ragu sauce recipe for instructions on preparing the sauce.

FRITTATA WITH ASPARAGUS | *Frittata con Asparagi*

INGREDIENTS

- 2 cups chopped asparagus
- ½ cup chopped parsley
- ¼ cup milk
- 6 eggs
- ½ cup Parmesan cheese
- 2 large cloves of garlic, diced
- ¼ cup extra virgin olive oil

INSTRUCTIONS

- ☐ Place half of the oil in a medium sauté pan.
- ☐ Add the asparagus to the pan.
- ☐ Sauté the asparagus until they are tender, being careful not to overcook.
- ☐ In a bowl, beat the eggs, Parmesan cheese, milk, and parsley.
- ☐ Add the egg mixture to the sautéed asparagus. Stir until well mixed.
- ☐ Lower the heat, cover the pan, and allow the frittata to cook slowly. Do not stir.
- ☐ When the sides and the top of the frittata look almost cooked, either flip the frittata onto a large plate or place it in the oven to finish cooking.
- ☐ Once done, let the frittata cool for a few minutes, then slice it into pizza-like slices and serve.

VEGETABLE FRITTATA | *Frittata di Verdure*

INGREDIENTS

- 1 whole onion, sliced
- 1 large red bell pepper, diced
- 2 good-sized zucchinis, diced
- 1 lb. of sliced fresh mushrooms
- 3 large garlic cloves, sliced small

- ½ cup chopped parsley
- 8 eggs
- ½ cup Parmesan cheese
- ¼ cup olive oil

INSTRUCTIONS

- ☐ Heat half of the oil in a medium sauté pan.
- ☐ Add garlic, onion, zucchini, mushrooms, and pepper to the pan.
- ☐ Sauté the vegetables until they are tender, making sure not to overcook them.
- ☐ Beat the eggs, Parmesan cheese, and parsley in a bowl.
- ☐ Add the egg mixture to the sautéed vegetables.
- ☐ Lower the heat, cover the pan, and allow the frittata to cook slowly. Do not stir.
- ☐ When the sides and the top of the frittata look almost cooked, either flip the frittata onto a large plate or place it in the oven to finish cooking.
- ☐ Once done, let the frittata cool for a few minutes, then slice it into pizza-like slices and serve.

ITALIAN VEGETABLE STEW | *Ciambotta*

INGREDIENTS

- 2 zucchinis (1 yellow and 1 green), cubed
- 3 Yukon gold potatoes, cubed
- 1 large onion, sliced
- 2 large carrots, sliced
- 2 stalks of celery, sliced
- 1 cup frozen peas
- 1 (32 oz.) low-sodium chicken broth

- 1 (28 oz.) can of San Marzano whole tomatoes (chopped or blended)
- 1 chicken bouillon cube
- ½ cup fresh basil, sliced
- 2 bay leaves
- Red pepper flakes (if desired)
- Extra virgin olive oil

INSTRUCTIONS

- ☐ Put all the sliced vegetables in separate bowls.
- ☐ Sauté the vegetables in the following order:
- ☐ In a large stock pot, heat about 3 tablespoons of oil.
- ☐ Add the zucchini and cook for about 10 minutes.
- ☐ Add the potatoes and cook for another 10 minutes.
- ☐ Add the onion and cook for another 10 minutes.
- ☐ Add the celery and carrots and cook for another 10 minutes.
- ☐ Add the tomatoes, peas, bouillon, bay leaf, and half of the basil.
- ☐ Cover the pot and allow the soup to slow cook for a couple of hours, stirring occasionally to ensure the vegetables don't overcook.
- ☐ Before serving, garnish the top with the remaining basil.
- ☐ If needed, add low-sodium chicken broth for extra liquid.
- ☐ Remember to remove the bay leaves before serving.
- ☐ Serve the soup with toasted sliced French bread and Parmesan cheese on the side.
- ☐ Season with salt and pepper to taste.

MIXED GREENS | *Minestra*

INGREDIENTS

- 1 bunch of collard greens
- 1 bunch of spinach
- 1 bunch of rapini (broccoli rabe)
- 1 bunch of mustard greens
- 1 bunch of dandelions
- 1 bunch of arugula
- 1 head of endive or escarole
- 1 tsp fennel seeds (optional)
- 1 large onion, diced
- 4 cloves of garlic, diced
- ¼ cup olive oil

INSTRUCTIONS

- ☐ Clean and cut each of the vegetables.
- ☐ In a large pot of boiling water, blanch the cut vegetables. Cook for about 10 minutes.
- ☐ Drain the blanched vegetables and set them aside.
- ☐ In a deep-frying skillet, heat the olive oil.
- ☐ Add the diced onion and garlic. Sauté until they are soft and translucent.
- ☐ Add the blanched vegetables to the skillet.
- ☐ If using, add the fennel seeds.
- ☐ Cook the mixture over medium-low heat for about 20 minutes, stirring occasionally. Avoid overcooking.

Tip: Serve as a side dish or pair it with a cornmeal pie (recipe page 92), as shown in the photo.

CORN MEAL PIE

INGREDIENTS

- 2 cups of cornmeal
- 2 tbsp white flour
- 3 cups of water
- 4 tbsp oil

INSTRUCTIONS

- ☐ Place the water in a small pan and bring it to a boil. Remove from the stove.
- ☐ Mix the white flour and cornmeal, and slowly stir the mixture into the hot water, adding a little at a time until it becomes nice and thick.
- ☐ Heat the oil in a small frying pan, then add the thickened cornmeal mixture. Press it into the pan to form a pie shape.
- ☐ Reduce the heat, cover the pan, and cook for about 30 minutes. Then, flip the pie over and return it to the frying pan to cook for another 30 minutes.
- ☐ Remove the pie from the pan and let it cool. Slice it into pieces like a pie.
- ☐ Serve the cornmeal pie with minestra.

MIXED GREENS WITH WHITE CANNELLINI BEANS | Verdi con Faggioli Cannellini

INGREDIENTS

- 3 tbsp of extra virgin olive oil
- 3 cloves of garlic, thinly sliced
- 3 or 4 bunches of fresh greens (see choices below)
- 1 (15.5 oz.) can of Cannellini beans
- Hot pepper flakes
- Black pepper
- Parmesan cheese (optional) to sprinkle on top

INSTRUCTIONS

- ☐ Clean the greens and roughly chop them. Blanch the greens and set them aside. Save ½ cup of the water used for blanching.
- ☐ Heat the olive oil in a medium-sized sauté pan. Add the blanched greens and ¼ cup of the saved blanching water. Cook for 3-4 minutes.
- ☐ Drain the Cannellini beans and add them to the greens, stirring well. Cook for 4-5 minutes, stirring occasionally.
- ☐ Transfer the mixture to a serving bowl.
- ☐ Add the thinly sliced garlic, toss everything together, and serve.
- ☐ Serve the dish with toasted Italian bread, pepper flakes, and Parmesan cheese (if desired).

Tip: This dish can be made with a mix of your favorite greens such as dandelion, spinach, mustard greens, curly endive, escarole, kale, and broccoli rabe (rapini). Additionally, if you prefer, you can use fresh beans. Follow the instructions on the package for soaking overnight and use them instead of canned beans in this dish.

LENTILS | *Lenticchie*

INGREDIENTS

- 1 (15 oz.) can of sweet peas
- 1 (19 oz.) can of Progresso Lentil Soup
- ¼ thin spaghetti, broken into inch pieces
- 1 cup low-sodium chicken broth
- 3 tbsp olive oil
- ¼ cup Parmesan cheese
- 1 can of mushrooms (if desired)

INSTRUCTIONS

- ☐ In a saucepan, empty the entire can of lentils.
- ☐ Add the entire can of peas along with its water.
- ☐ If using, add the entire can of mushrooms along with its water.
- ☐ Add the olive oil.
- ☐ Pour in 1 cup of low-sodium chicken broth.
- ☐ Bring the mixture to a boil and let it simmer for about 5 minutes.
- ☐ Add the broken pieces of thin spaghetti and bring the mixture back to a boil. Simmer for 15 to 20 minutes or until the spaghetti is fully cooked.
- ☐ If needed, add more chicken broth to reach your desired consistency.
- ☐ Serve the soup, garnishing it with Parmesan cheese.

94

RISOTTO

INGREDIENTS

- 6 cups chicken stock (low sodium can be used)
- 1 onion, sliced
- 1 lb. Portobello or cremini mushrooms, sliced
- ½ cup dry white wine
- 2 tbsp butter
- 1 ½ cups Arborio rice
- Extra virgin olive oil
- Parmesan cheese
- Diced parsley or chives for sprinkling on top

INSTRUCTIONS

- ☐ In a pan, sauté the mushrooms and onion until they turn golden.
- ☐ Add the rice, stir well, and cook for about 5 minutes.
- ☐ Stir in the butter.
- ☐ Pour in the white wine and let it cook down.
- ☐ Add the chicken stock and stir thoroughly. Lower the heat, cover the pan, and allow it to simmer for about 20 minutes, stirring occasionally.
- ☐ Transfer the risotto to a serving dish.
- ☐ Top the dish with grated Parmesan cheese and a sprinkle of parsley or chives.

If you prefer, you can follow Aunt Carolina's recipe for the risotto, on page 96.

95

AUNT CAROLINA'S RISOTTO RECIPE

INGREDIENTS

- 1 cup diced carrots
- 1 cup diced celery
- ½ cup diced parsley
- 4 cups chicken stock
- 1 cup of sliced mushrooms

- 1 sliced onion
- 1 lb. ground sausage
- ½ cup ground chicken livers (optional)
- 1 ½ cups of Arborio rice

INSTRUCTIONS

☐ Combine the diced carrots, celery, parsley, and chicken stock in a pot. Cook until the vegetables are just about tender. Set aside and allow them to cool.

☐ In another pan, sauté the following ingredients in a little bit of olive oil: sliced mushrooms, sliced onion, ground sausage, ground chicken livers (optional), and Arborio rice.

☐ Stir until all the ingredients are well mixed and the rice is almost translucent.

☐ Incorporate the cooked vegetables and chicken stock into the pan.

☐ Cover the pan and let the mixture simmer for about 20 minutes, stirring occasionally. The rice should become nice and creamy as it cooks.

☐ Transfer the risotto to a serving dish.

☐ Sprinkle Parmesan cheese on top and garnish with diced parsley or chives.

SAUTEED GOURMET MUSHROOMS | *Funghi Fritti*

INGREDIENTS

- 1 ½ lbs. oyster mushrooms
- 1 ½ lbs. cremini mushrooms
- 4 large garlic cloves, sliced
- ½ cup white wine
- Garlic powder
- Salt and pepper, to taste
- Red pepper flakes (if desired)

INSTRUCTIONS

- ☐ Wash and clean the mushrooms. Place them in a medium stock pan.
- ☐ Bring the mushrooms to a boil and let them boil for about 15 minutes
- ☐ Drain the mushrooms and set them aside.
- ☐ In a frying skillet, add the oil and the sliced garlic.
- ☐ Cook the garlic until it becomes nice and golden. Remove the garlic from the pan and set it aside in a small bowl.
- ☐ Add the mushrooms to the hot oil, stir, and begin to fry them. Pour in the white wine, and add a little garlic powder, salt, and pepper to taste.
- ☐ Cover the skillet, lower the heat to medium, and cook for about half an hour.
- ☐ Uncover the skillet and continue cooking for another half an hour, allowing the excess juice to drain.
- ☐ Place the cooked garlic back into the skillet, stir, and cook for an additional 5-10 minutes.
- ☐ Turn off the stove and allow the mushrooms to sit in the pan until ready to serve.
- ☐ When ready to serve, gently reheat the mushrooms and place them in a serving bowl.

Tip: You can use additional kinds of gourmet mushrooms or mixed dried gourmet mushrooms. If using dried gourmet mushrooms, be sure to follow the preparation instructions before frying them.

SAUTEED STRING BEANS | *Fagiolini Saltati*

INGREDIENTS

- 1 lb. fresh string beans
- 1 (14.5 oz.) can of stewed Italian tomatoes (chopped in a blender)
- 1 tbsp oregano
- 3 garlic cloves, diced
- Extra virgin olive oil
- Salt and pepper, to taste

INSTRUCTIONS

- ☐ Clean and blanch the string beans, then set them aside.
- ☐ In a medium saucepan, add a couple of tablespoons of olive oil.
- ☐ Sauté the diced garlic in the oil until it becomes golden.
- ☐ Add the chopped tomatoes and oregano to the saucepan.
- ☐ Cook the tomato mixture for about 2-3 minutes.
- ☐ Add the blanched string beans to the pan. Mix well to coat the beans with the tomato sauce. Cover the pan and cook until the beans are tender.
- ☐ Salt and pepper to suit your preferences.

PAN-FRIED ZUCCHINI | *Zucchini fritti all'aceto*

INGREDIENTS

- 2 nice-sized zucchinis, sliced ⅛ of an inch
- ½ cup extra virgin olive oil

- 2 cloves of garlic, diced
- ¼ cup fresh mint, diced
- Salt and pepper, to taste

INSTRUCTIONS

- ☐ Heat the olive oil in a skillet.
- ☐ Fry the zucchini slices until they turn golden. Place them on a paper towel to drain.
- ☐ Layer the fried zucchini in a serving dish, adding a little diced garlic and mint between the layers.
- ☐ Once finished, drizzle some oil, mint, and vinegar over the top for a final touch.
- ☐ Set the dish aside until ready to serve. Before serving, gently toss the salad to mix the flavors.
- ☐ Salt and pepper to suit your preferences.

ZUCCHINI WITH PARMESAN CHEESE |
Zucchini con Parmigiano

INGREDIENTS

- 1 large zucchini, sliced (about ½-inch thick)
- 1 cup fresh Parmesan cheese
- 1 cup water

INSTRUCTIONS

- ☐ In a medium skillet, add water.
- ☐ Place the sliced zucchini in the skillet
- ☐ Cover the skillet and cook over low heat for about 15 minutes or until the zucchini is just about done.
- ☐ Turn off the heat and drain the water.
- ☐ Cover the zucchini with the Parmesan cheese.
- ☐ Cover the skillet again and let it stand.
- ☐ Serve the dish hot.

PEAS AND ONIONS | *Piselli e cipolle*

INGREDIENTS

- 1 lb. bag of frozen peas
- 1 medium onion, sliced
- 4 tbsp extra virgin olive oil
- Salt and pepper to taste

INSTRUCTIONS

- ☐ In a skillet, sauté the onions until they are softened.
- ☐ Add the peas to the skillet and mix them well with the onions.
- ☐ Cover the skillet and cook for about 10 to 15 minutes.
- ☐ Serve as a side dish.

CHEESE

Formaggio Fresco

FRESH CHEESE | *Formaggio Fresco*

INGREDIENTS

▸ **2 gallons of whole milk**

▸ **8 junket tablets (crushed)**

DIRECTIONS

- ☐ Place the milk in a large pot.
- ☐ Heat 3 tablespoons of milk in a small bowl in the microwave, just to warm it up.
- ☐ Add the crushed junket tablets to this small bowl and mix until they are melted.
- ☐ Put the melted tablets in the large pot of milk.
- ☐ Stir until well blended.
- ☐ Cook the milk on very low heat.
- ☐ Place a slotted ladle in the milk, partially cover it, and let it slow cook.
- ☐ DO NOT STIR.
- ☐ The milk will slowly start to jell. This process takes a couple of hours.
- ☐ Check every once in a while, but do not stir.
- ☐ The milk will begin to gel and form a hard gel at the top.
- ☐ When it has finally become a solid piece on the top, begin to spoon the cheese out slowly.
- ☐ Put it in a cheese basket with a bowl under the basket, as the water will begin to drip out while the cheese begins to form in the basket.

- ☐ Repeat this process until all of the cheese is out. You may need more than one cheese basket.
- ☐ Press the top of the cheese when placing in the baskets to help drain the water.
- ☐ Let them drain for about an hour before placing them in the refrigerator.
- ☐ Once there is less drainage or hardly any, cover the baskets with plastic wrap or tin foil and place them in the refrigerator.
- ☐ Keep them in the refrigerator for 24 hours, checking every once in a while to see if it is still draining and dump the water out.
- ☐ The cheese should be firm the next day. Flip the basket upside down onto a small serving plate.
- ☐ If it's hard to take out, run a spatula around the edges of the basket to loosen it up.
- ☐ Don't worry if it breaks a little bit.
- ☐ Serve it as a side dish with salami and other cheeses. Add crackers or sliced French bread to spread the cheese on.
- ☐ Use salt and pepper to taste.

Tip: This cheese is also used in the filling for Pizza Piena (Easter Pie); the recipe is on page 46.

103

LAPIO

PATRIA DEL FIANO

LAPIO (AVELLINO), CAMPANIA

Nestled on the Tyrrhenian Sea's shores, Campania is a southern Italy region between the tranquil Garigliano River and the Gulf of Policastro. It encompasses the provinces of Avellino, Benevento, Caserta, Napoli, and Salerno.

THE REGION IS MOUNTAINOUS AND HILLY to the north, with the infamous Mt. Vesuvius in the center. As a result, the land there is fertile due to the volcanic soil and produces some of the country's best tomatoes and fruits, such as figs, peaches, oranges, and lemons. Campania is also known for the famous Mozzarella di Bufala and ricotta and sheep's milk Pecorino.

Within one of the provinces, Avellino, is a town called Lapio. Surrounding towns are Taurasi, San Mango sul Calore, Montemiletto, Luogosano, and Chiusano di San Domenico.

Situated in a valley on the left bank of the Calore River near Mount Tuoro, Lapio is an agricultural center in the heart of Irpinia. The name may be derived from the Latin "lapideum," meaning rocky or stony, or from Apia, a variety of grapes already known in Roman times. The Patron Saint is San Pietro Martire, celebrated on April 29th. From 1000, the town followed the events linked to the Filangieri family, who owned it for about seven centuries, until 1806, when feudalism was abolished.

WHAT TO SEE IN LAPIO:

SANTA CATERINA CHURCH with a beautiful stone portal and a bell tower on the side of the façade.

THE PALAZZO BARONALE. Residence of the Filangieri family from the 16th century.

THE CHURCH OF CARMINE. The church of Santa Maria della Neve. Begun in 1600, the present construction goes back to the beginning of the century. Inside the church are kept paper pulp statues symbolizing religious figures of the New Testament. On Easter, they are exhibited to the public during Holy Week.

THE CONVENT OF SANTA MARIA DEGLI ANGELI. The ruins of the ancient religious complex can be seen in the area called Le Marmore.

WINE CALLED FIANO DI LAPIO. The winery there is one of the best white grapes in Italy. It grows particularly well in the hilly Lapio-Arianello region. It is considered one of the most prized locations for the Fiano grape.